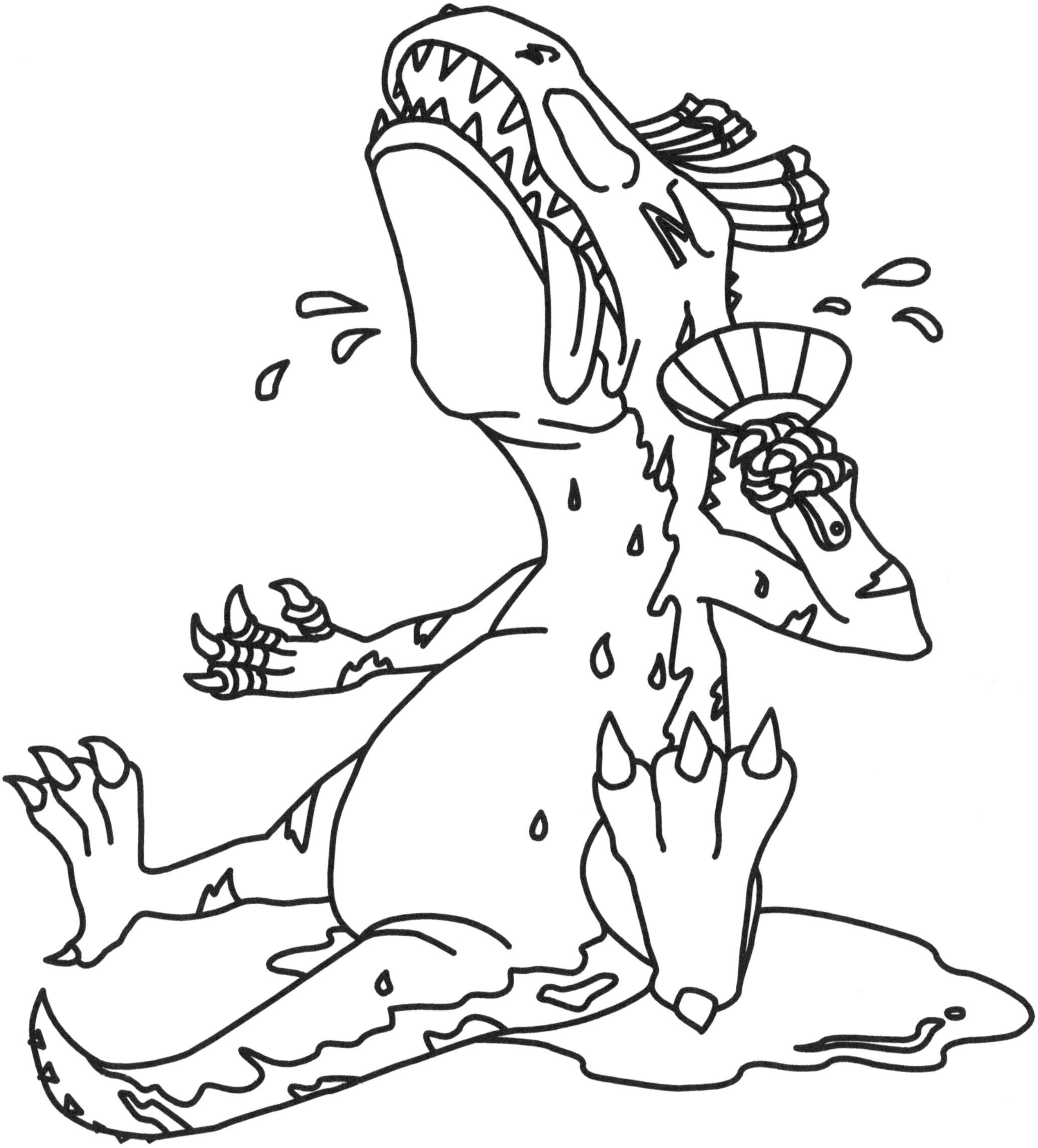

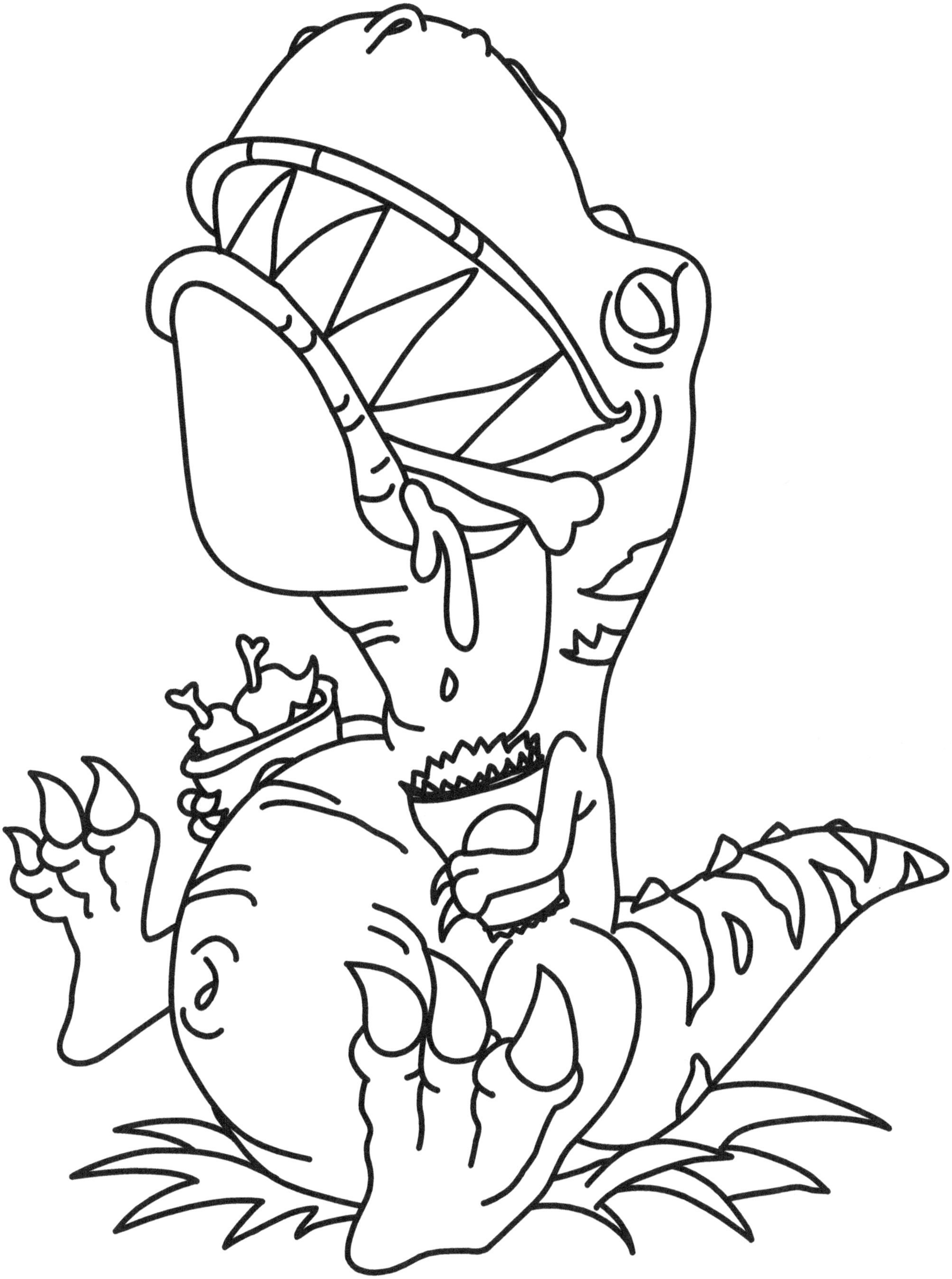

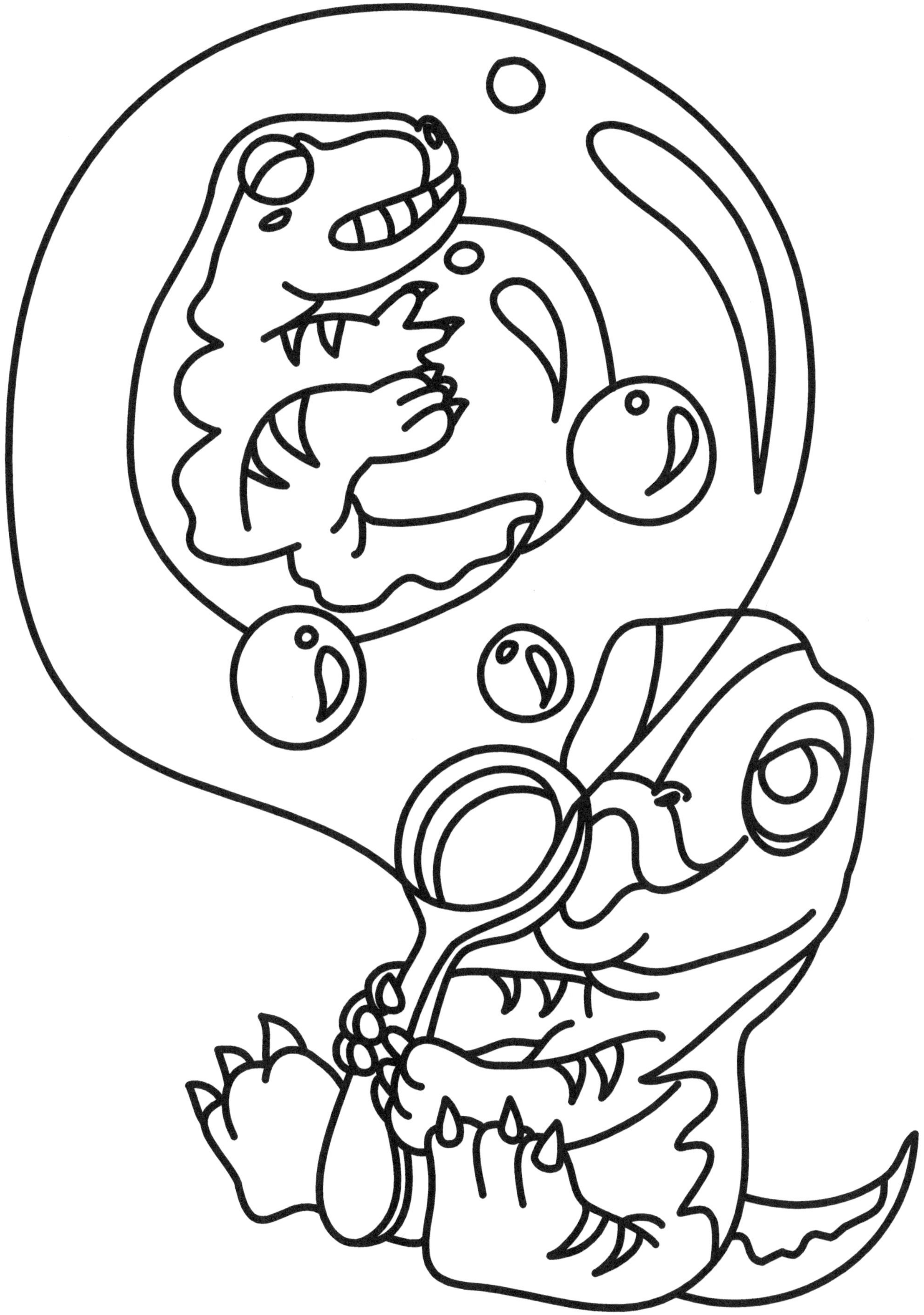

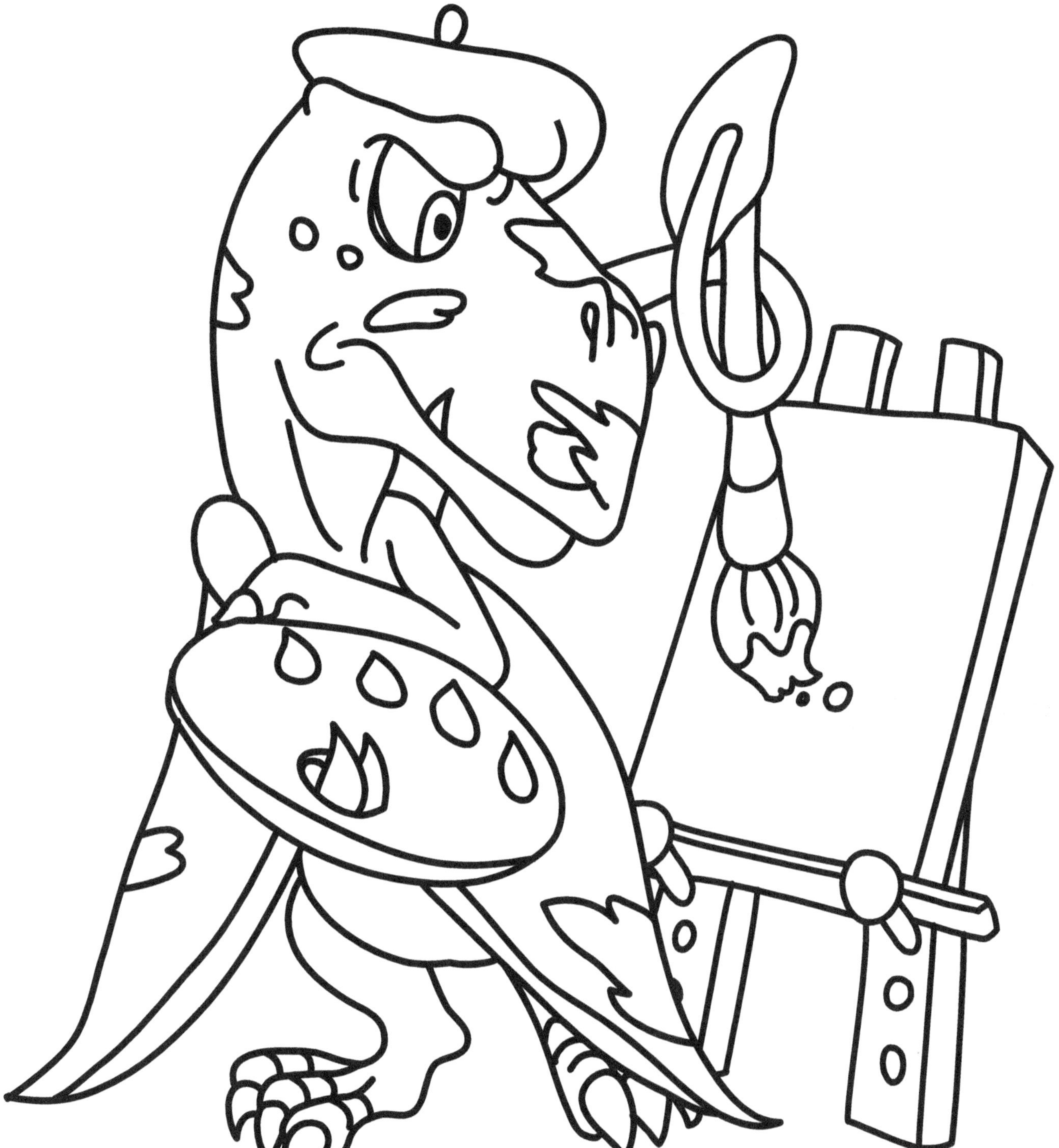

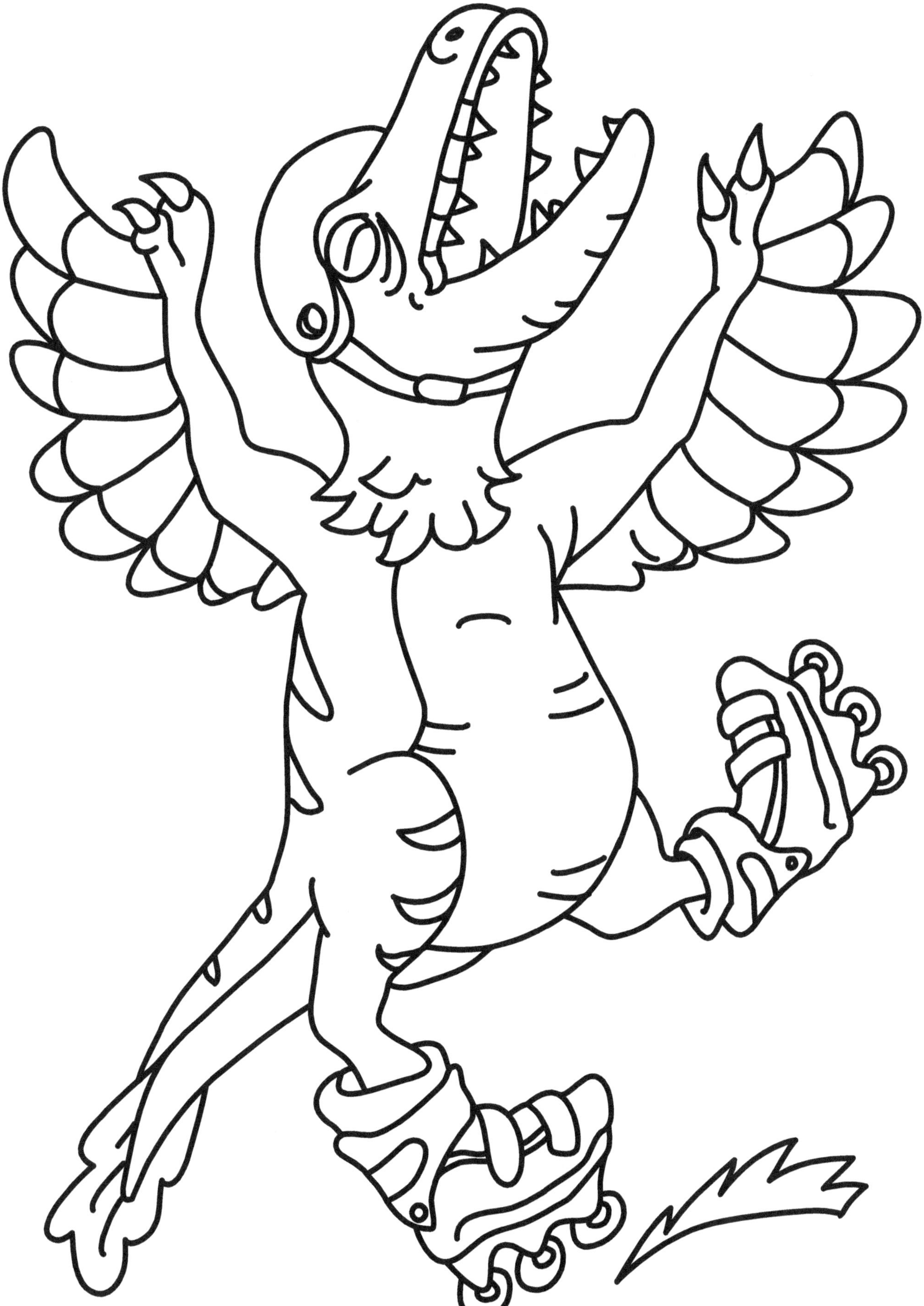

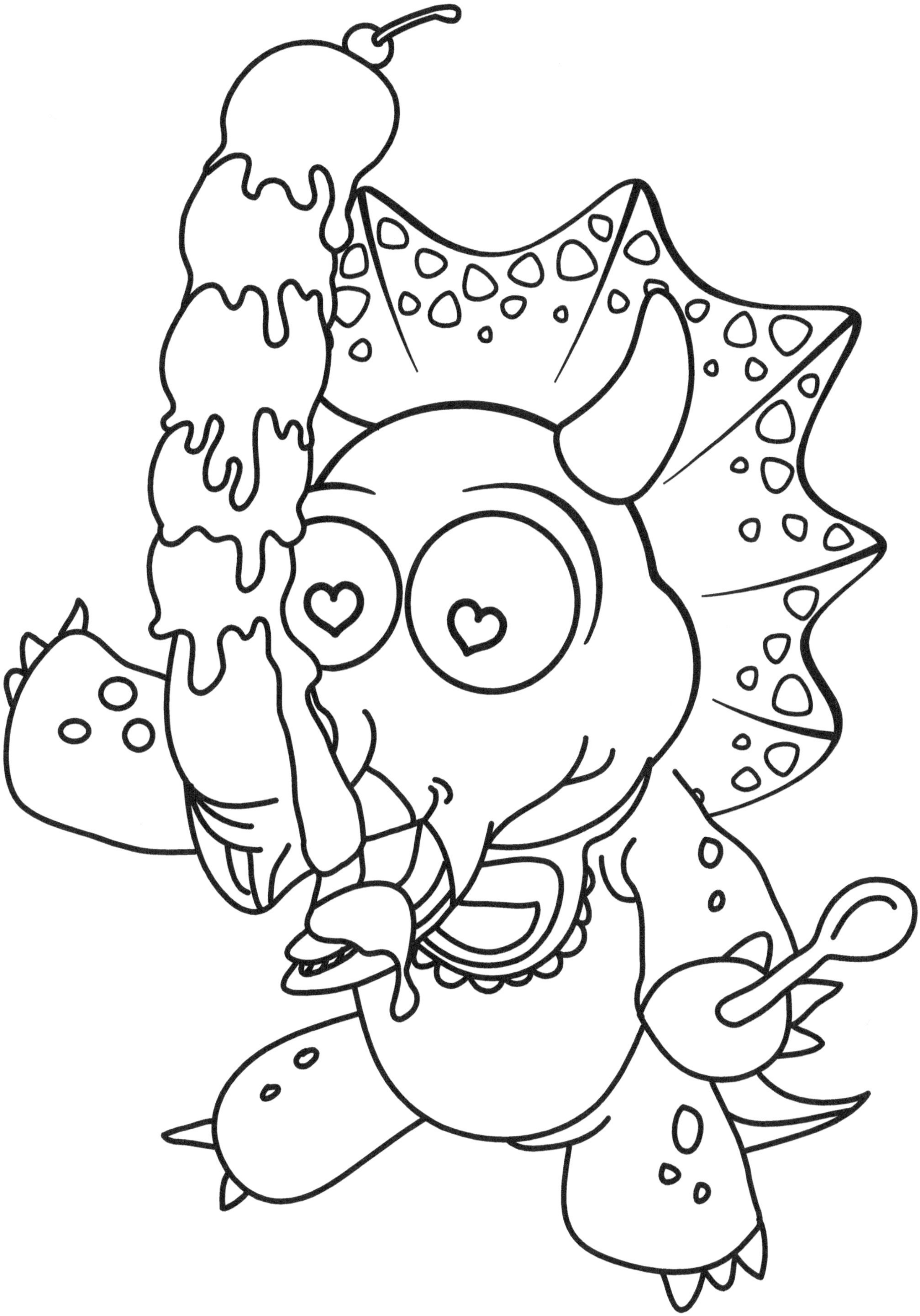

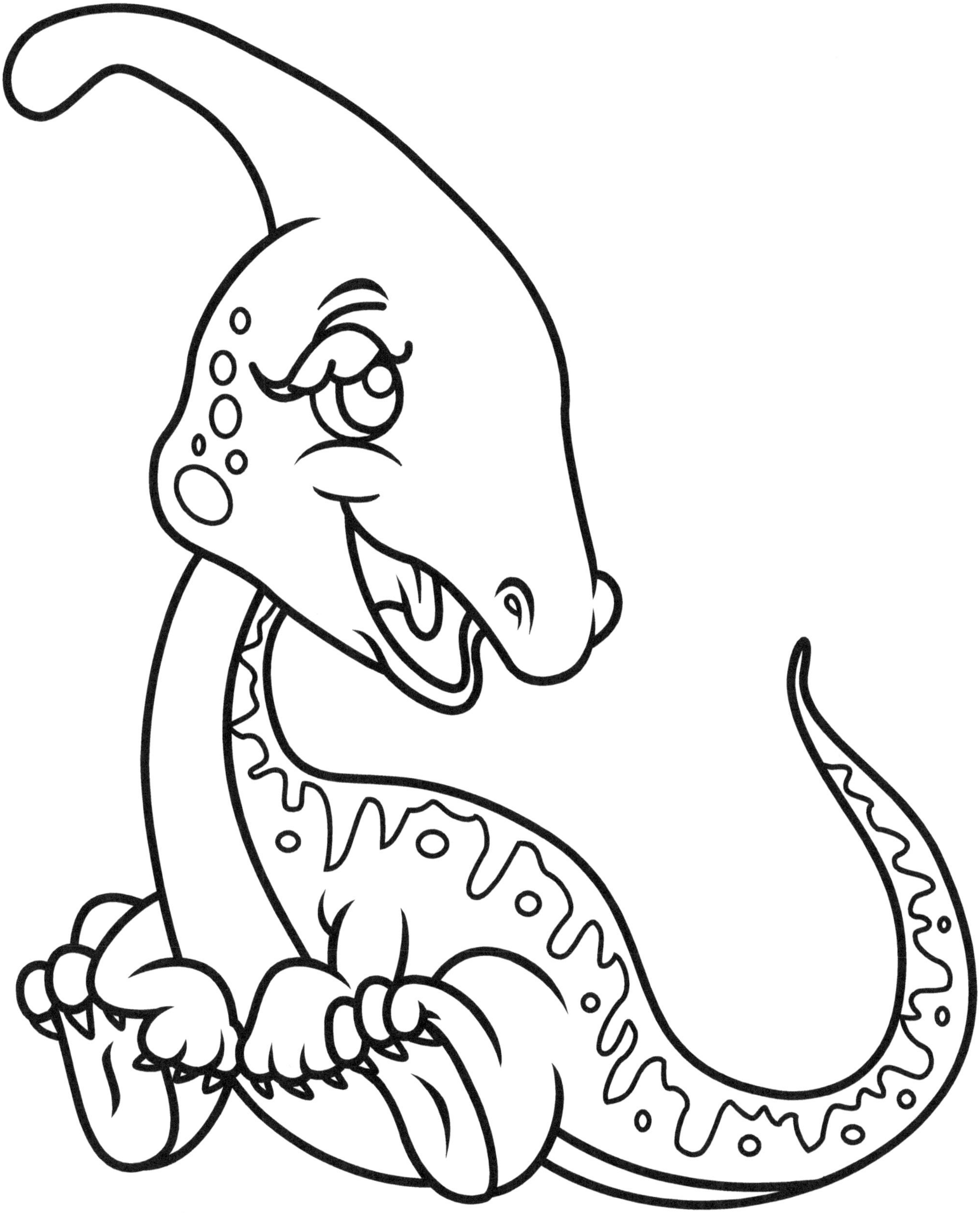

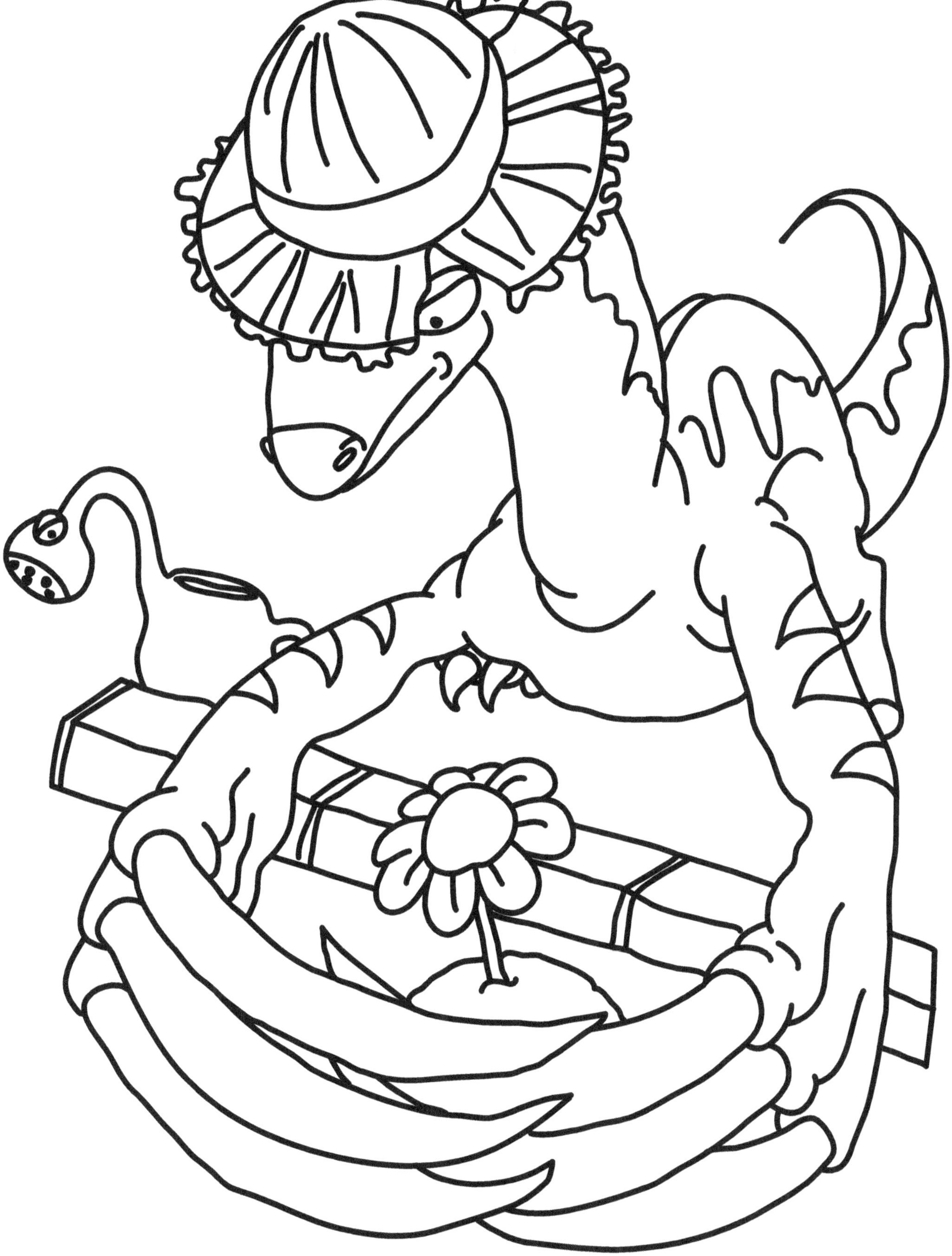

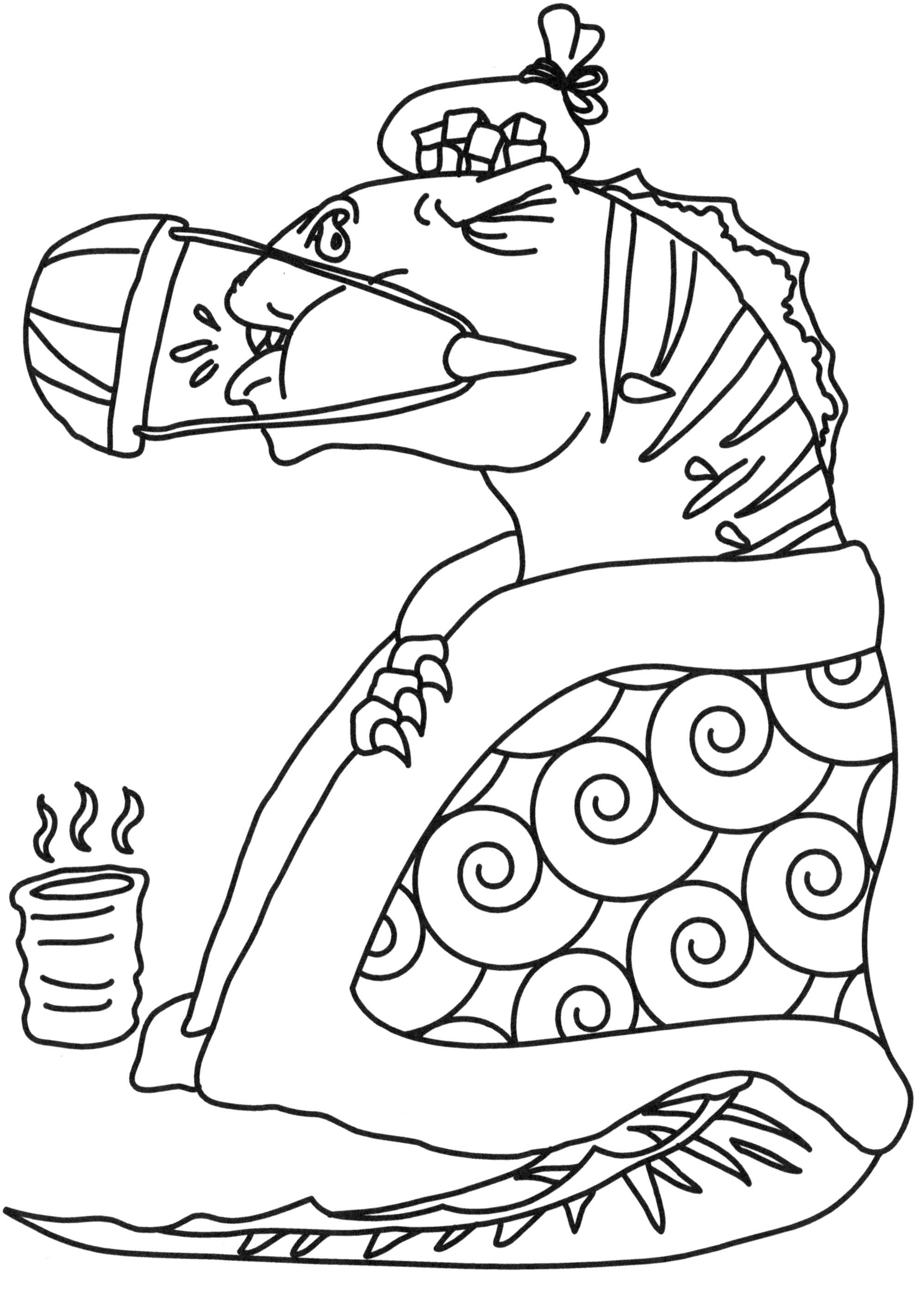

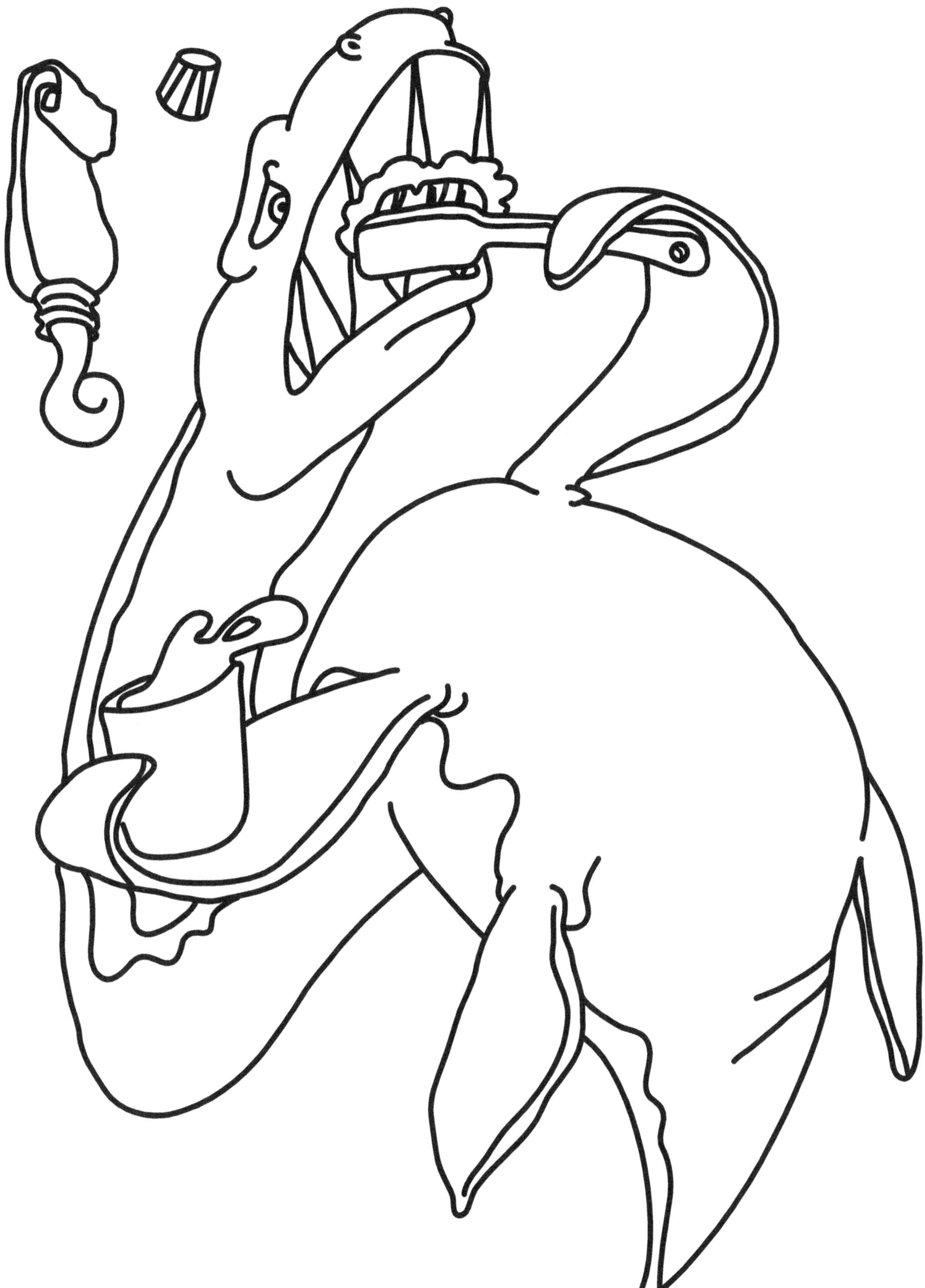

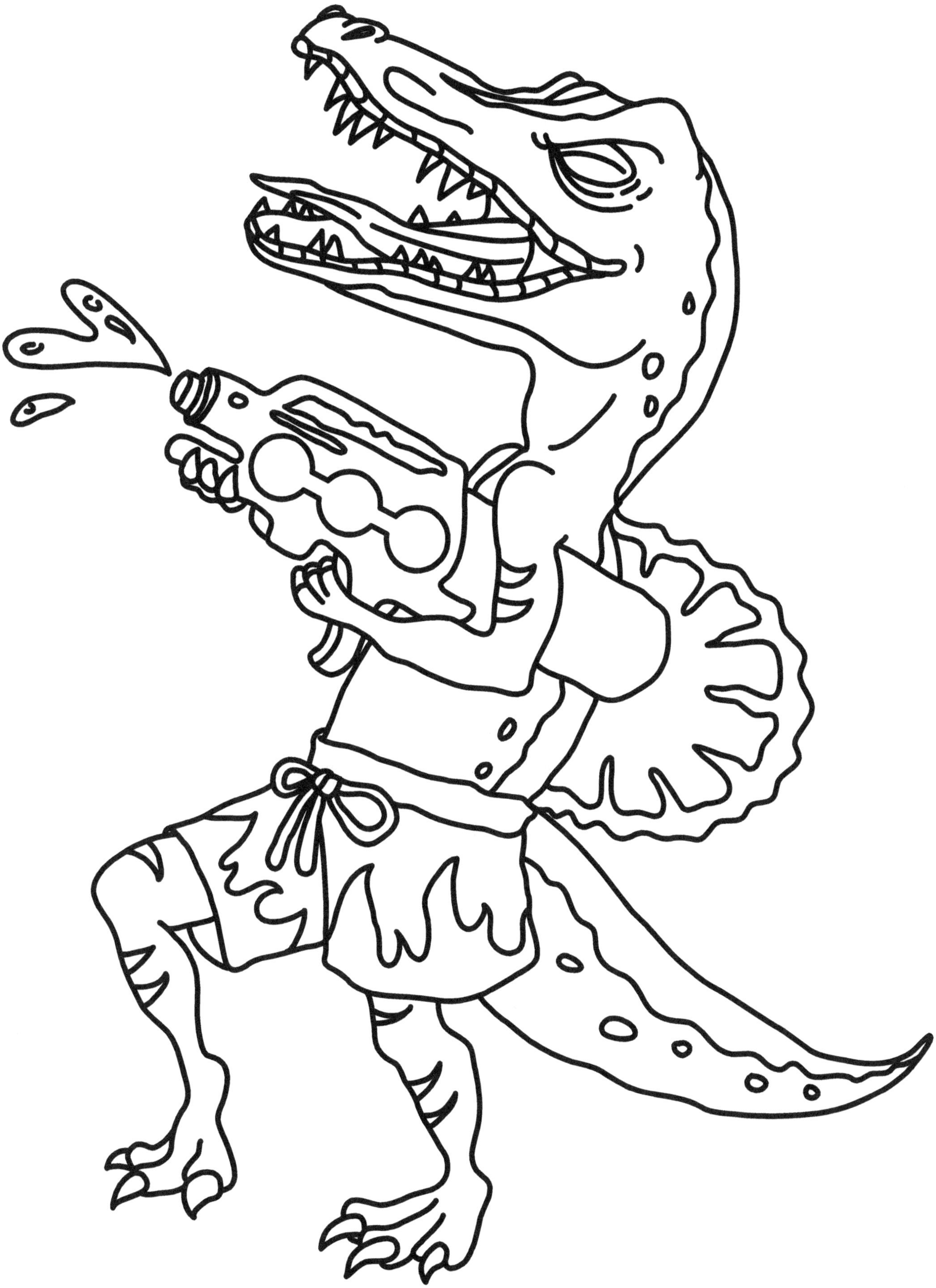

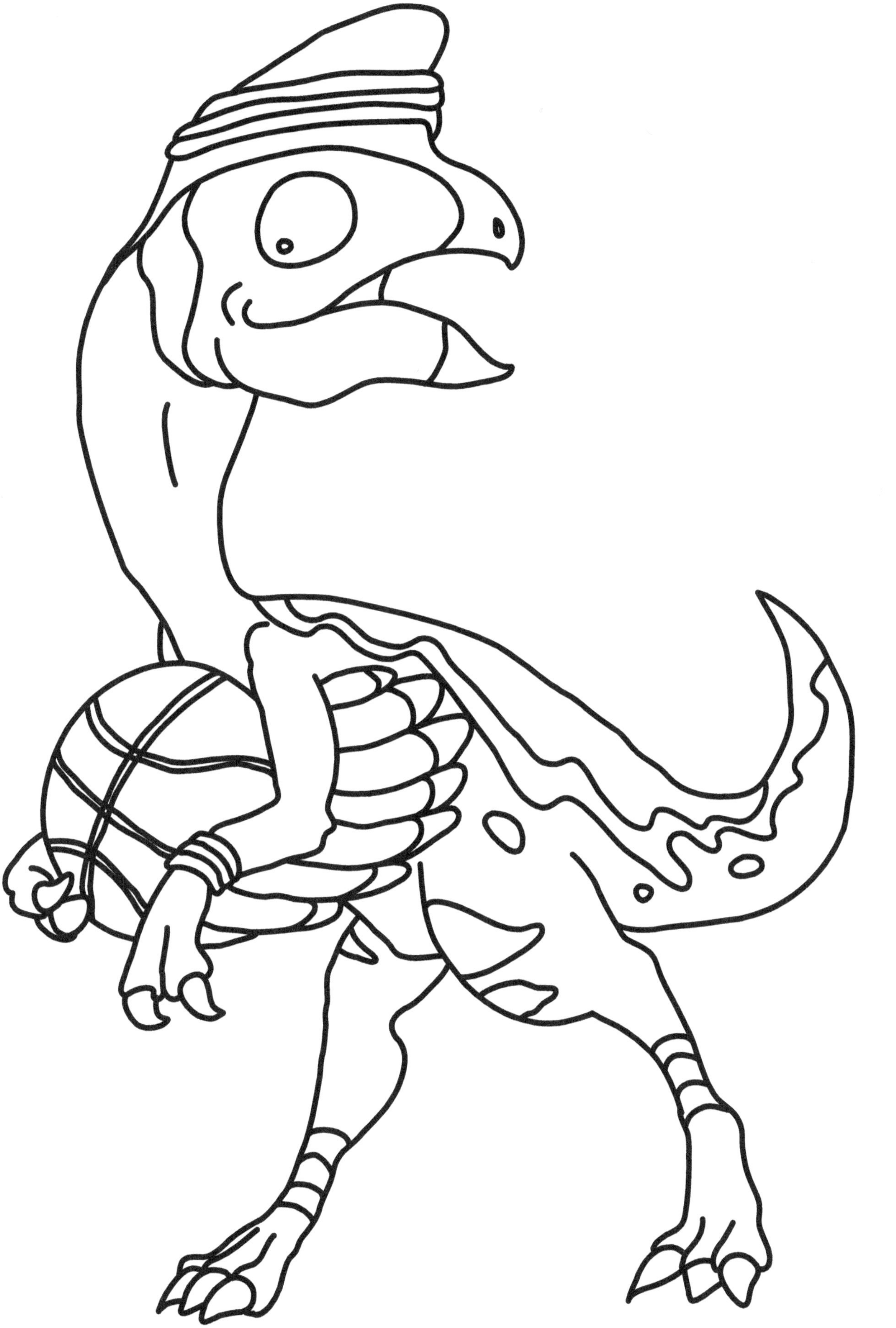

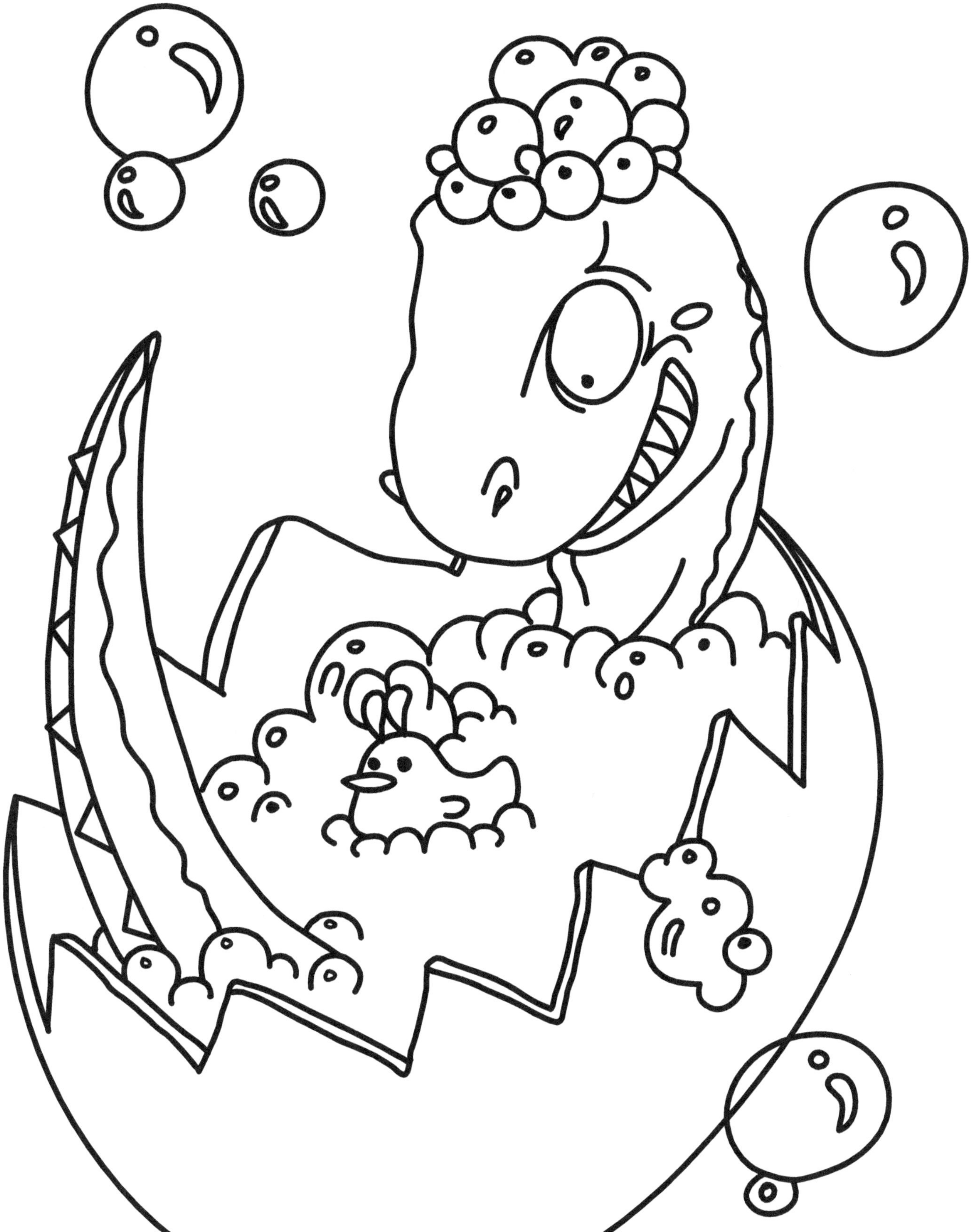

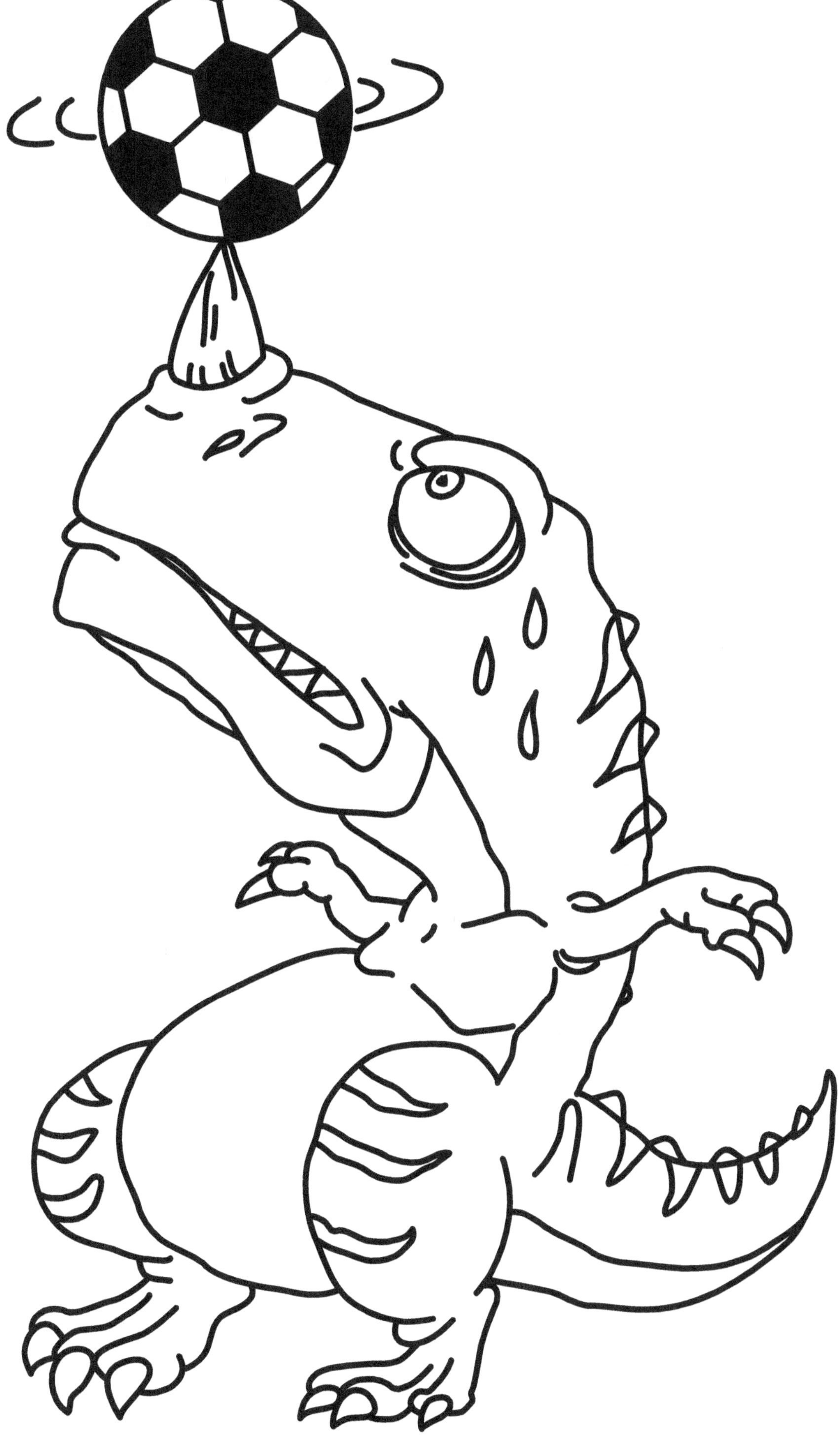

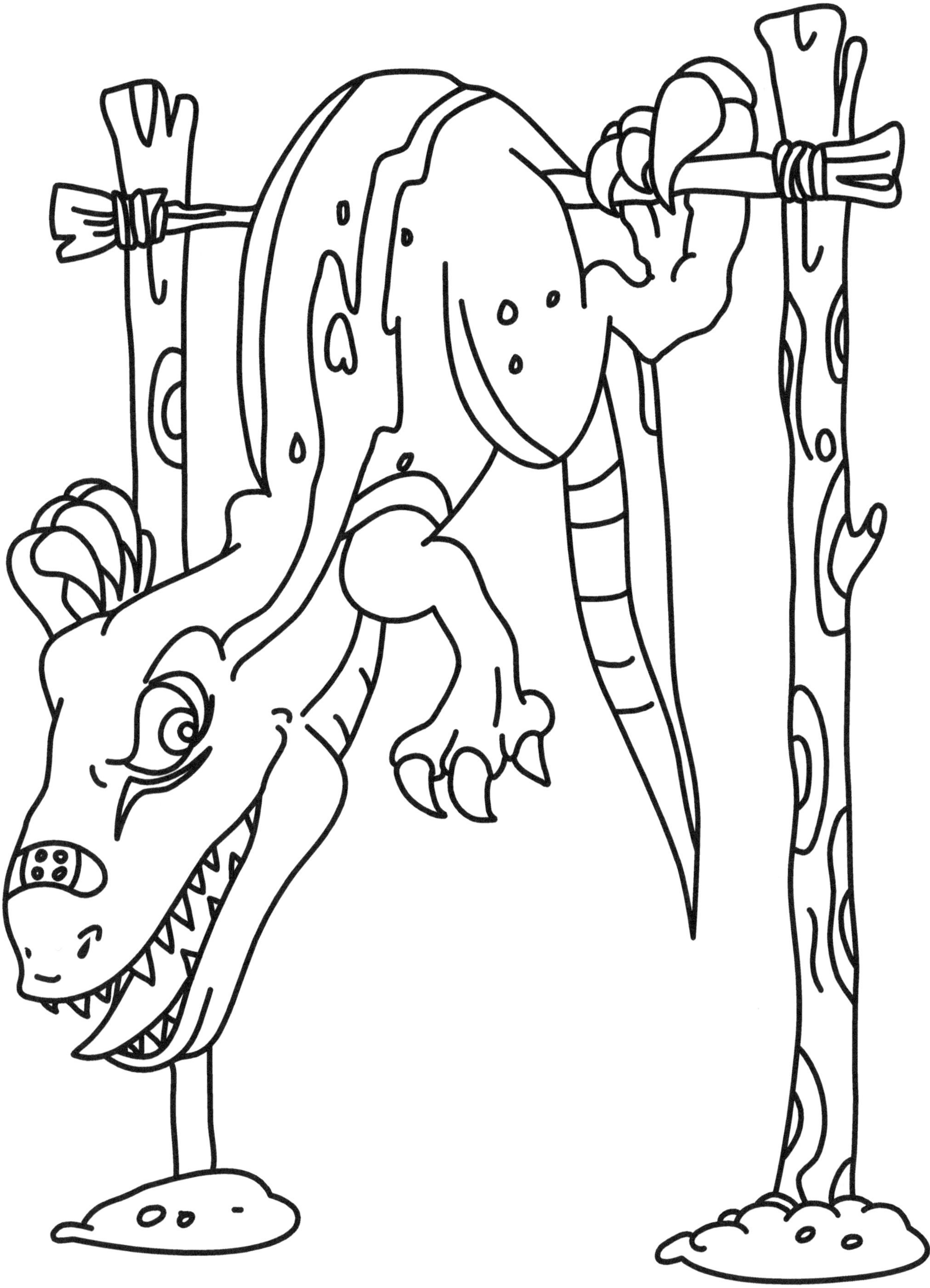

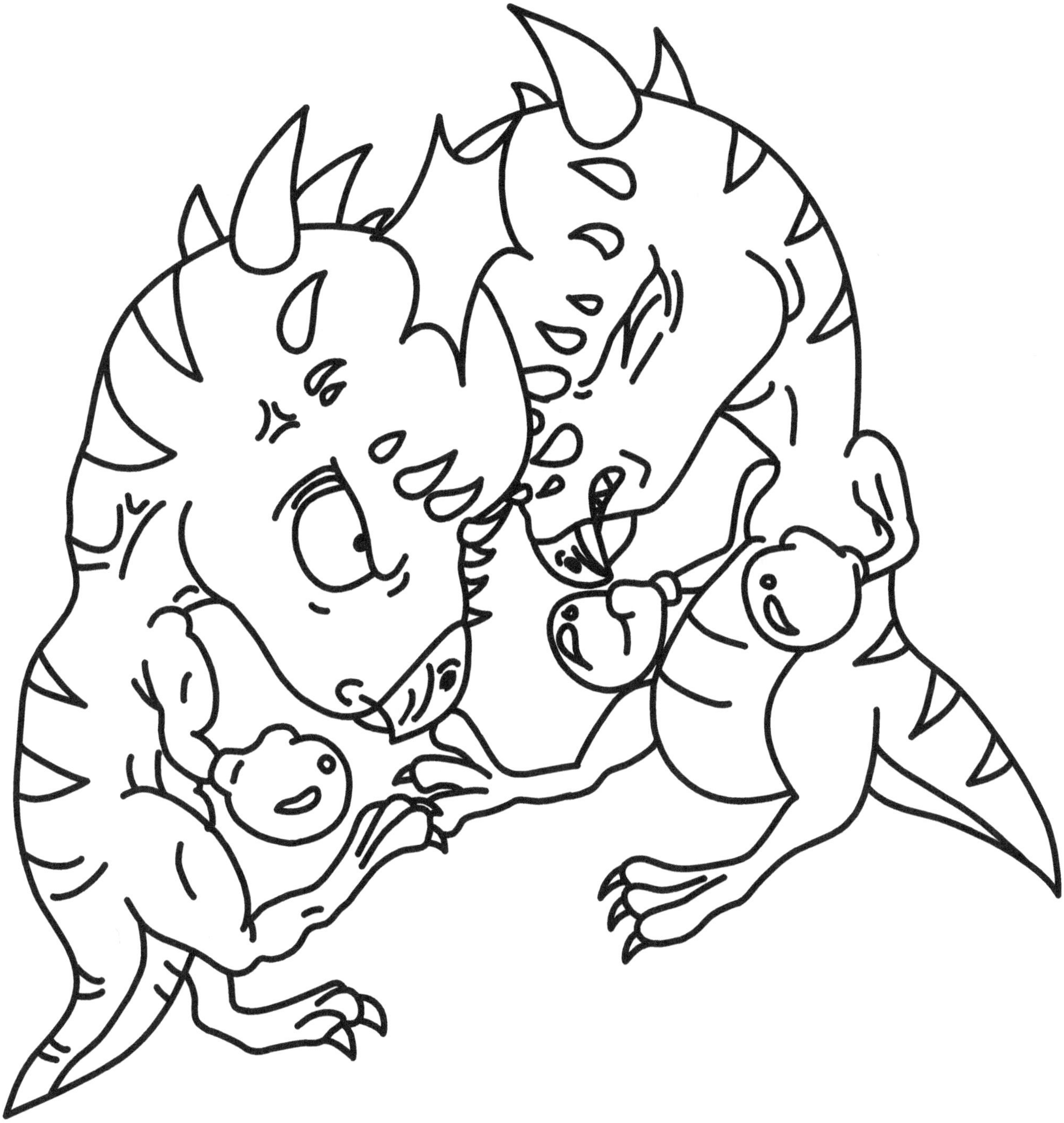

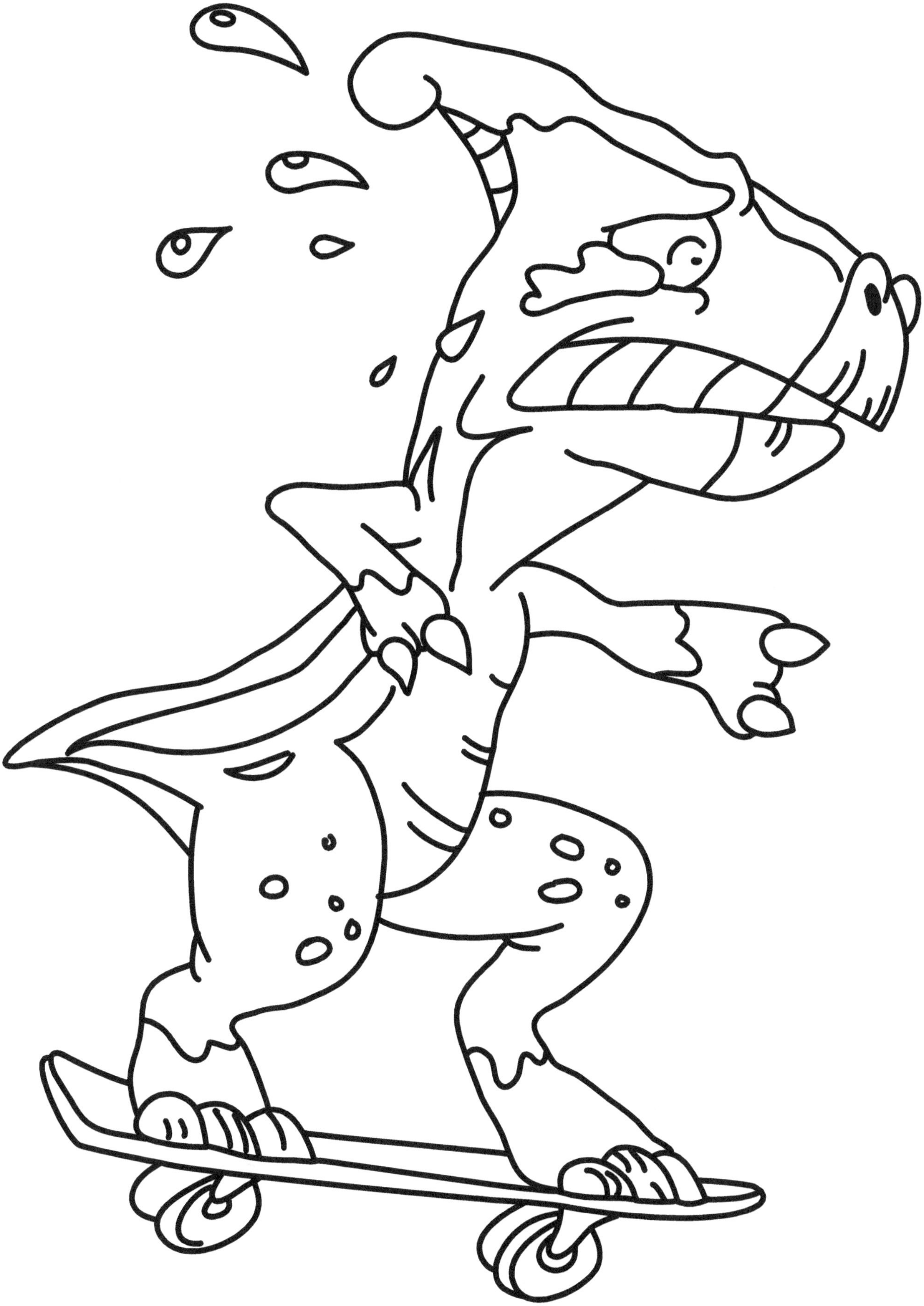

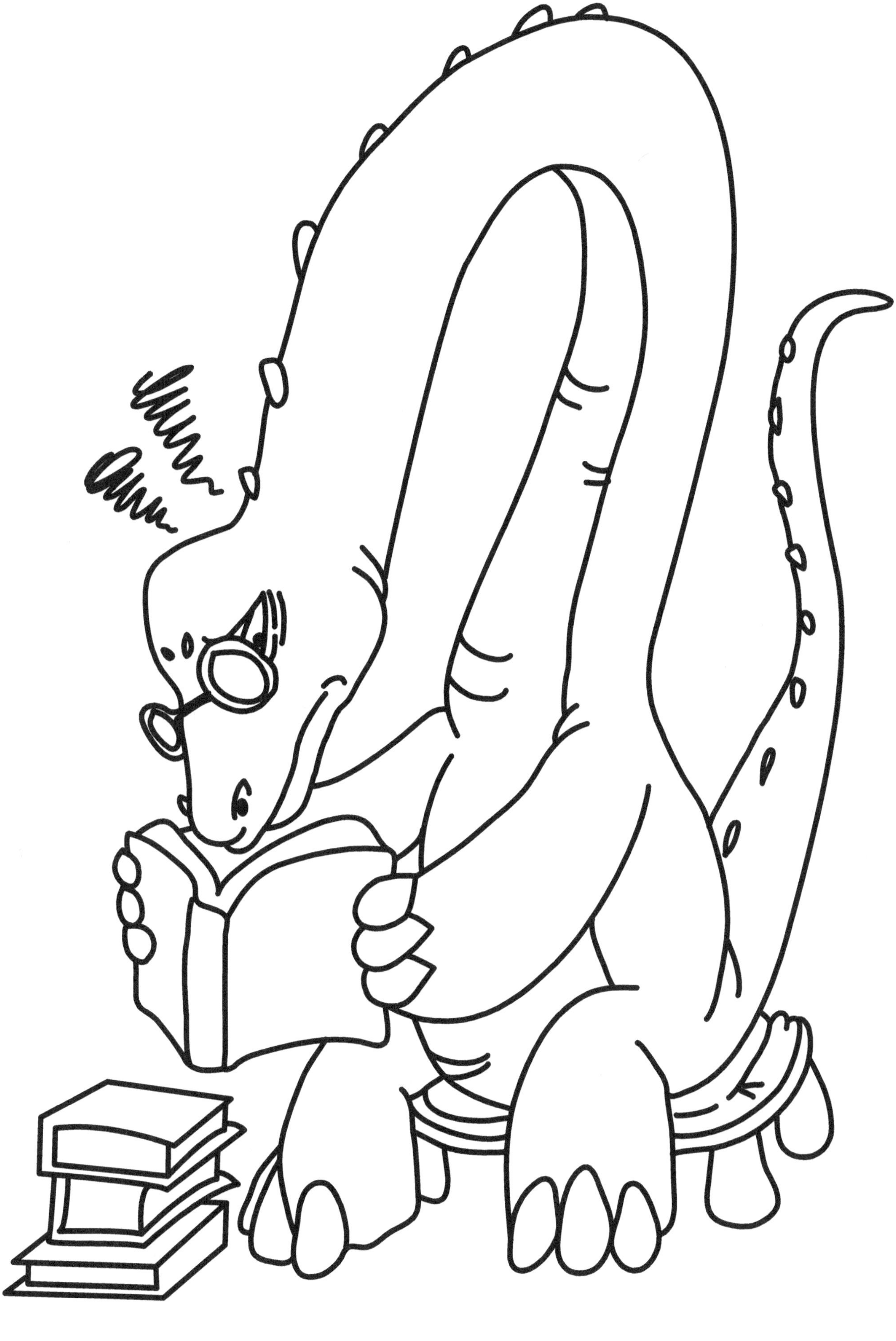

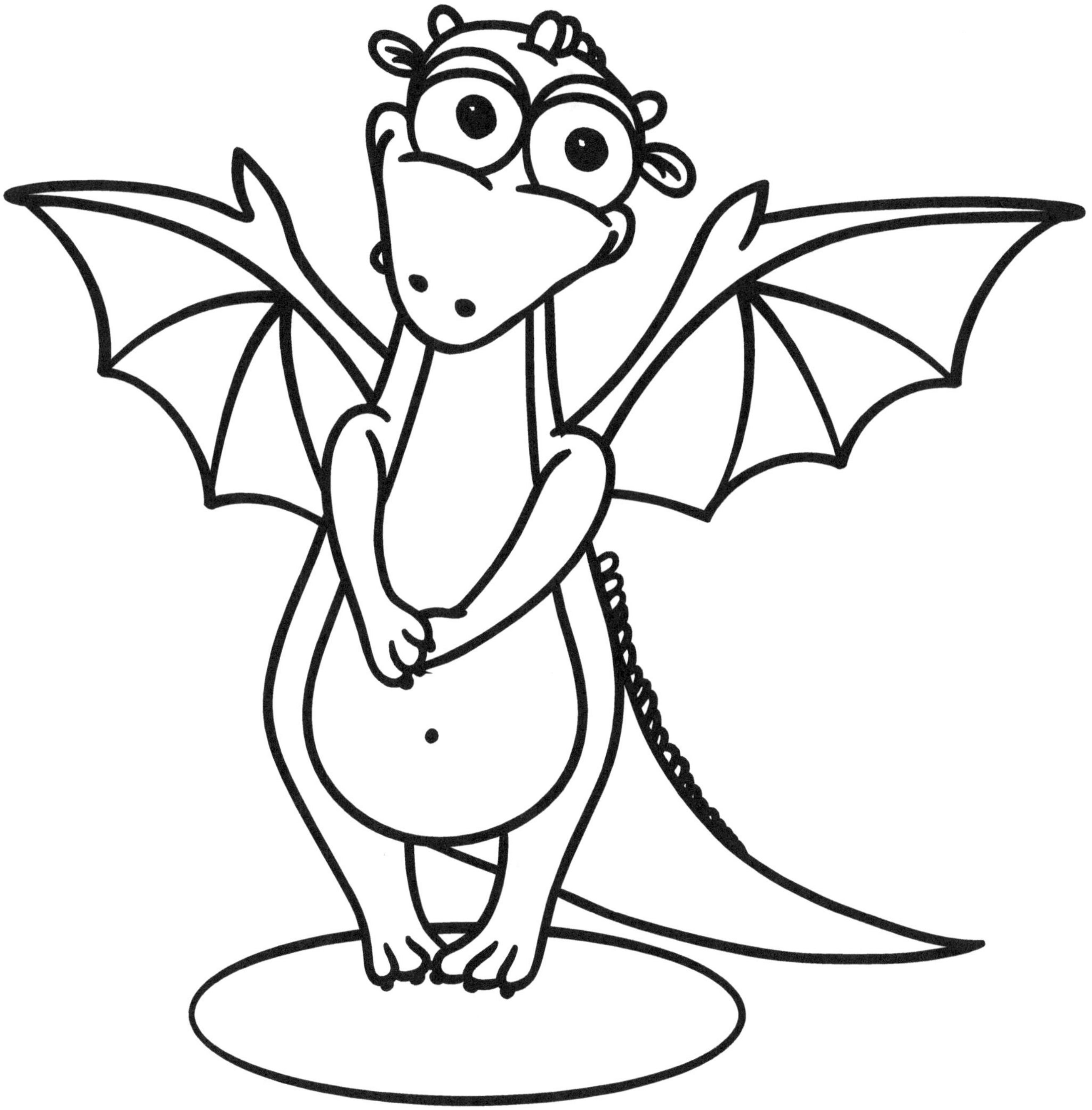

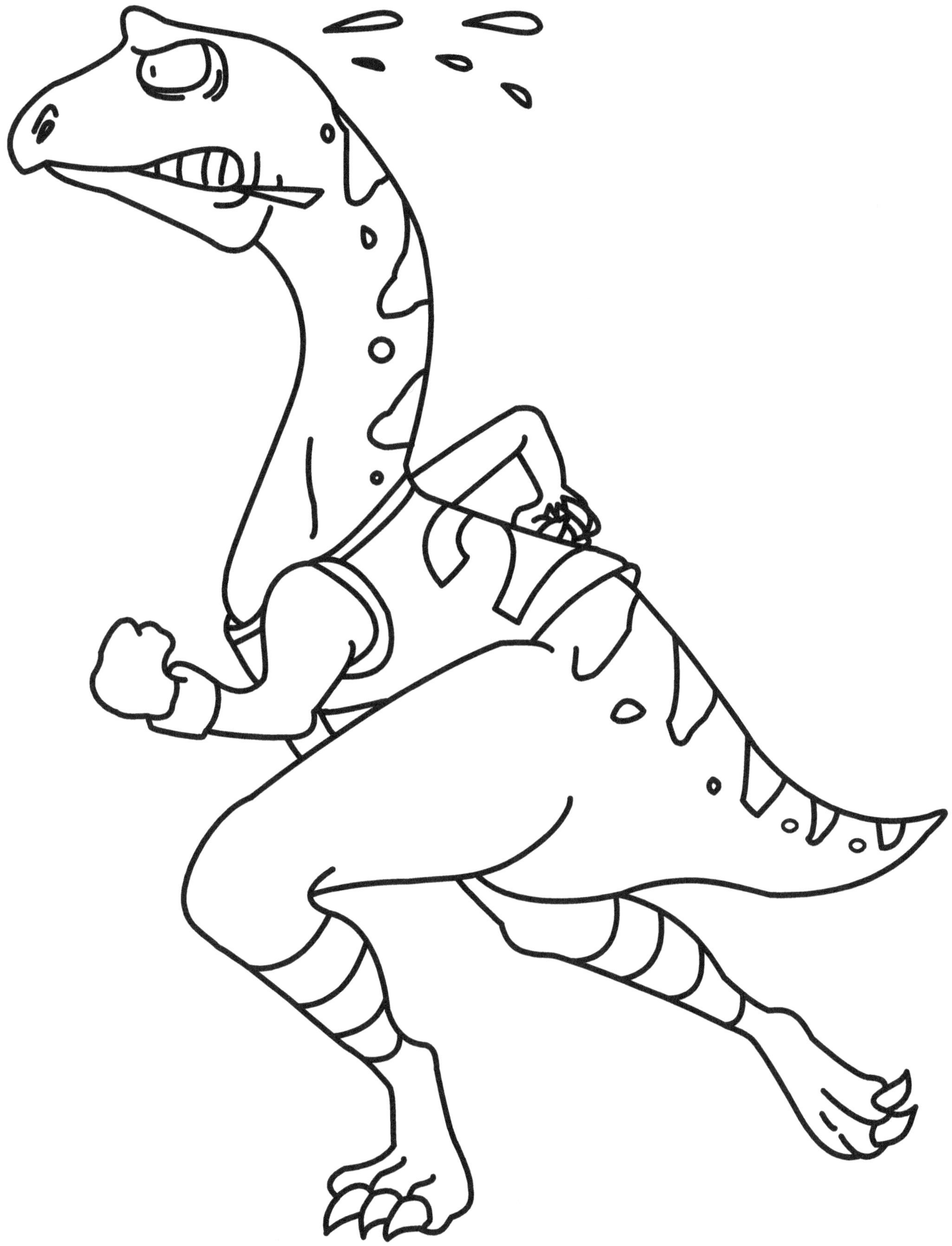

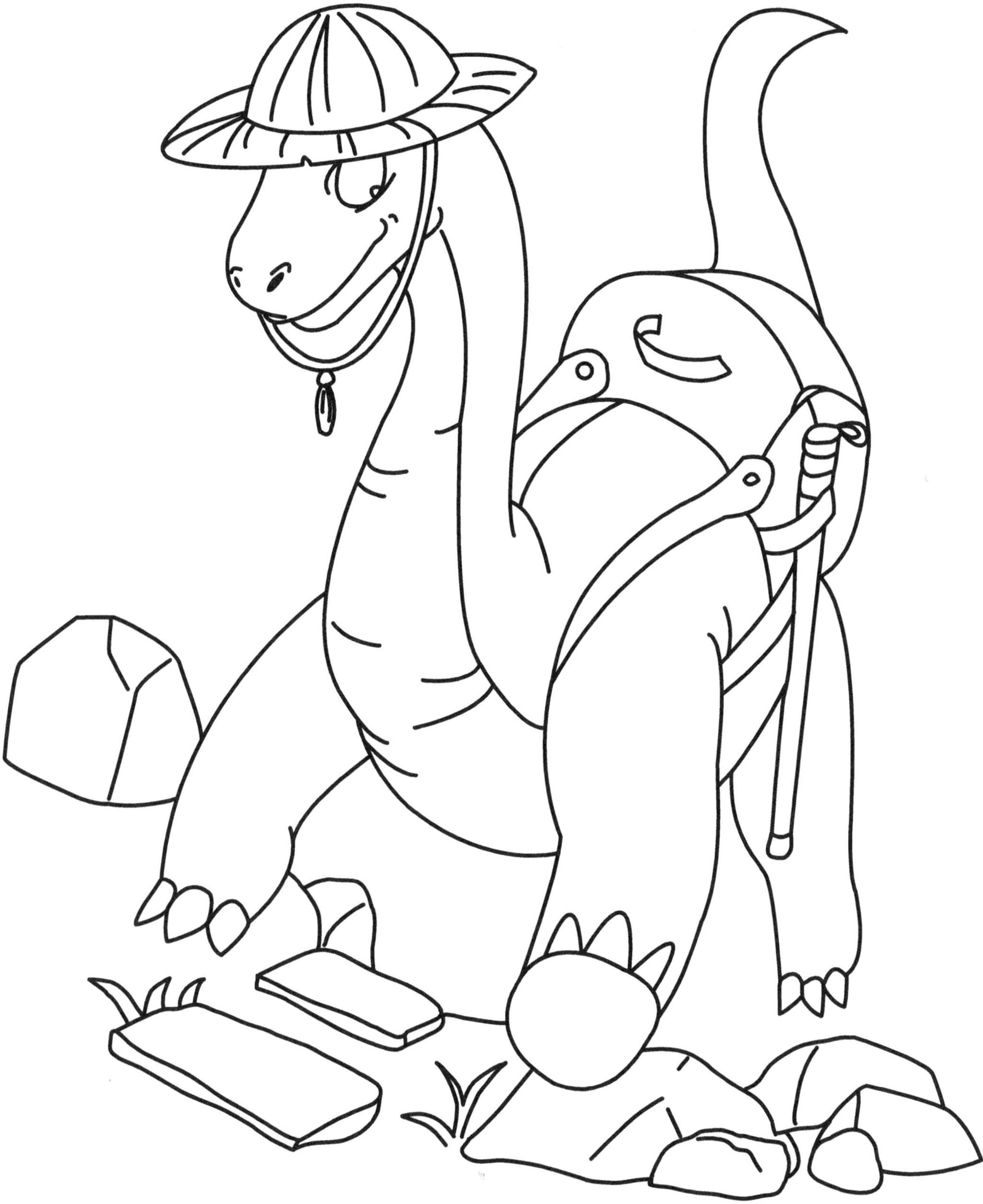

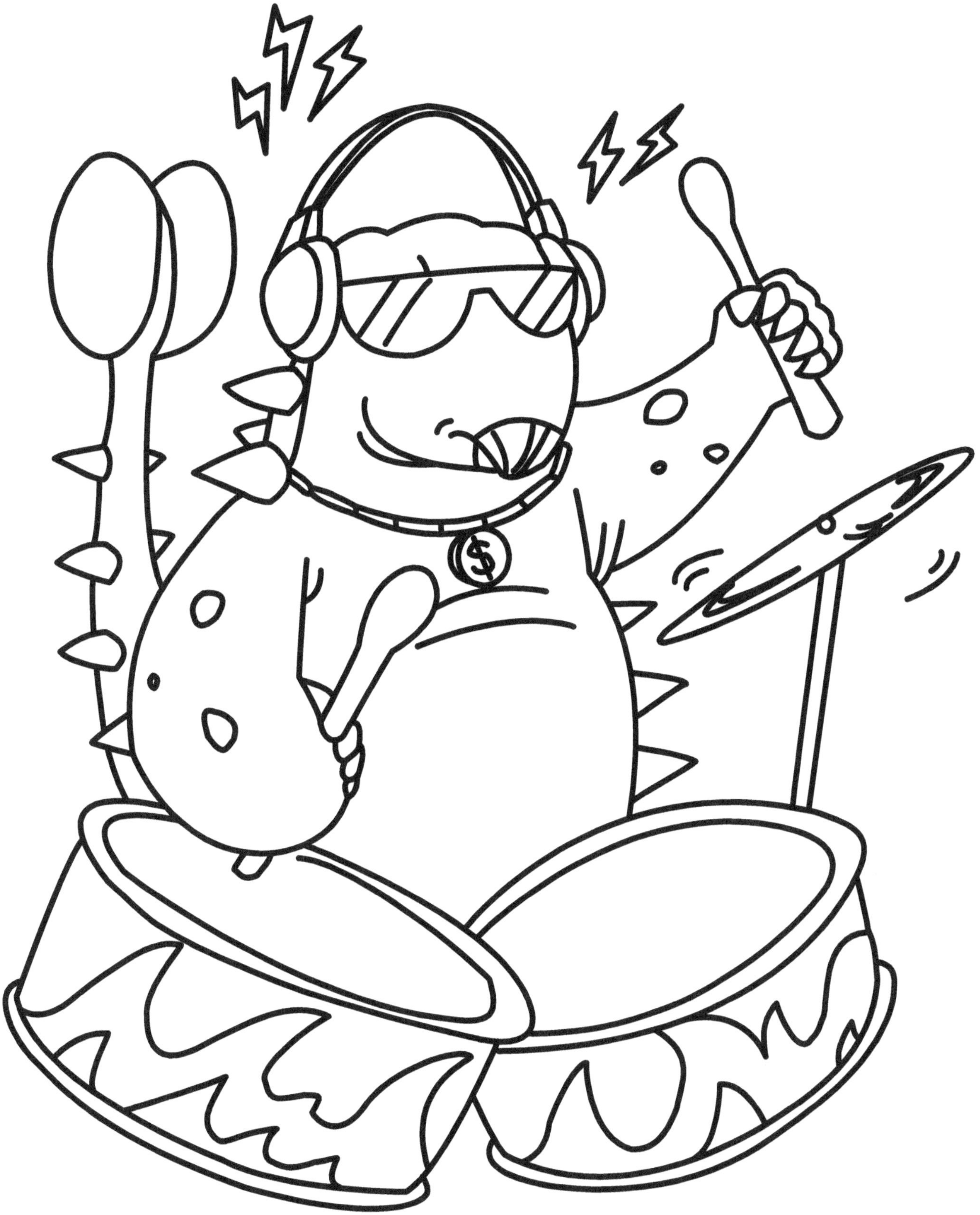

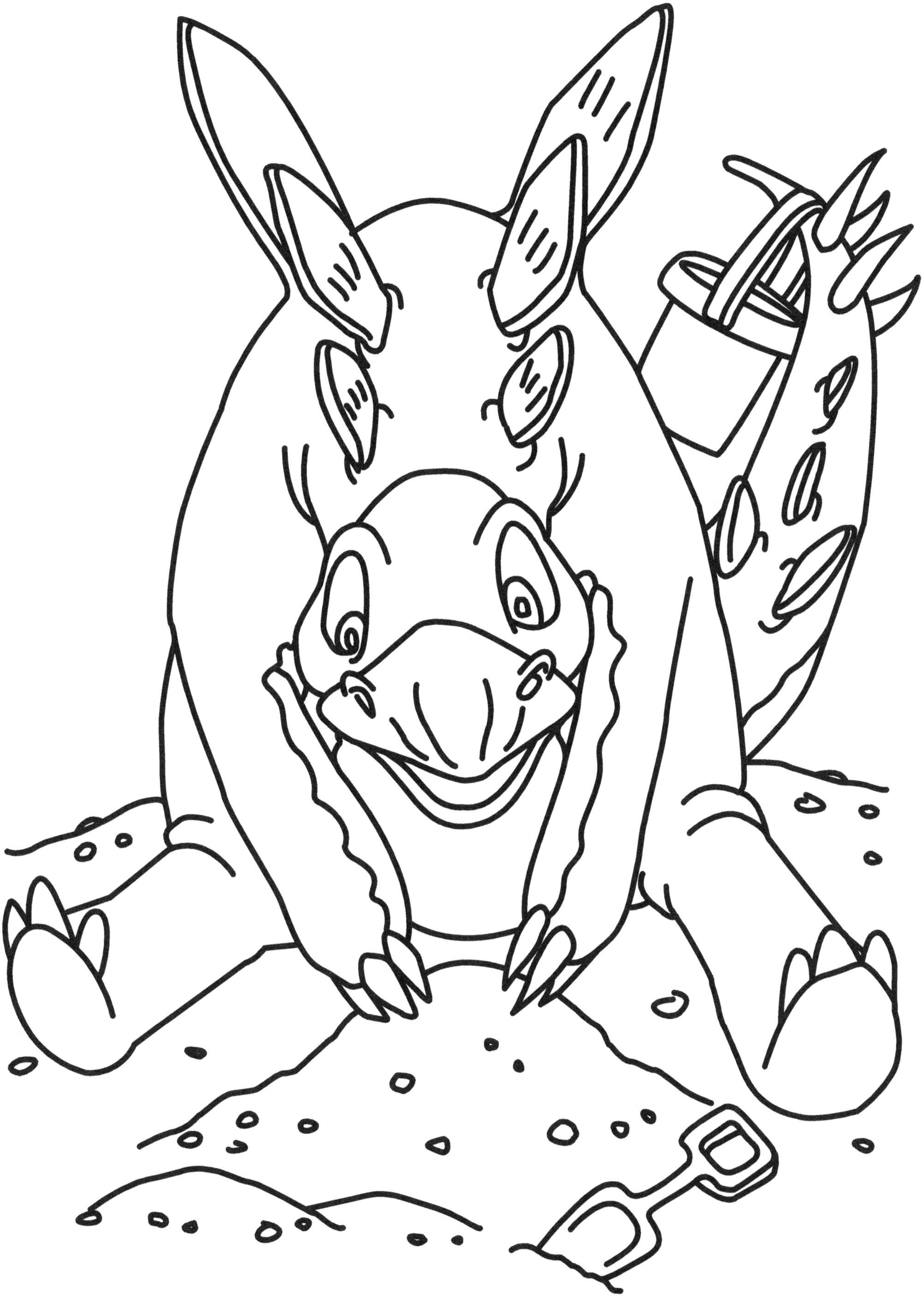

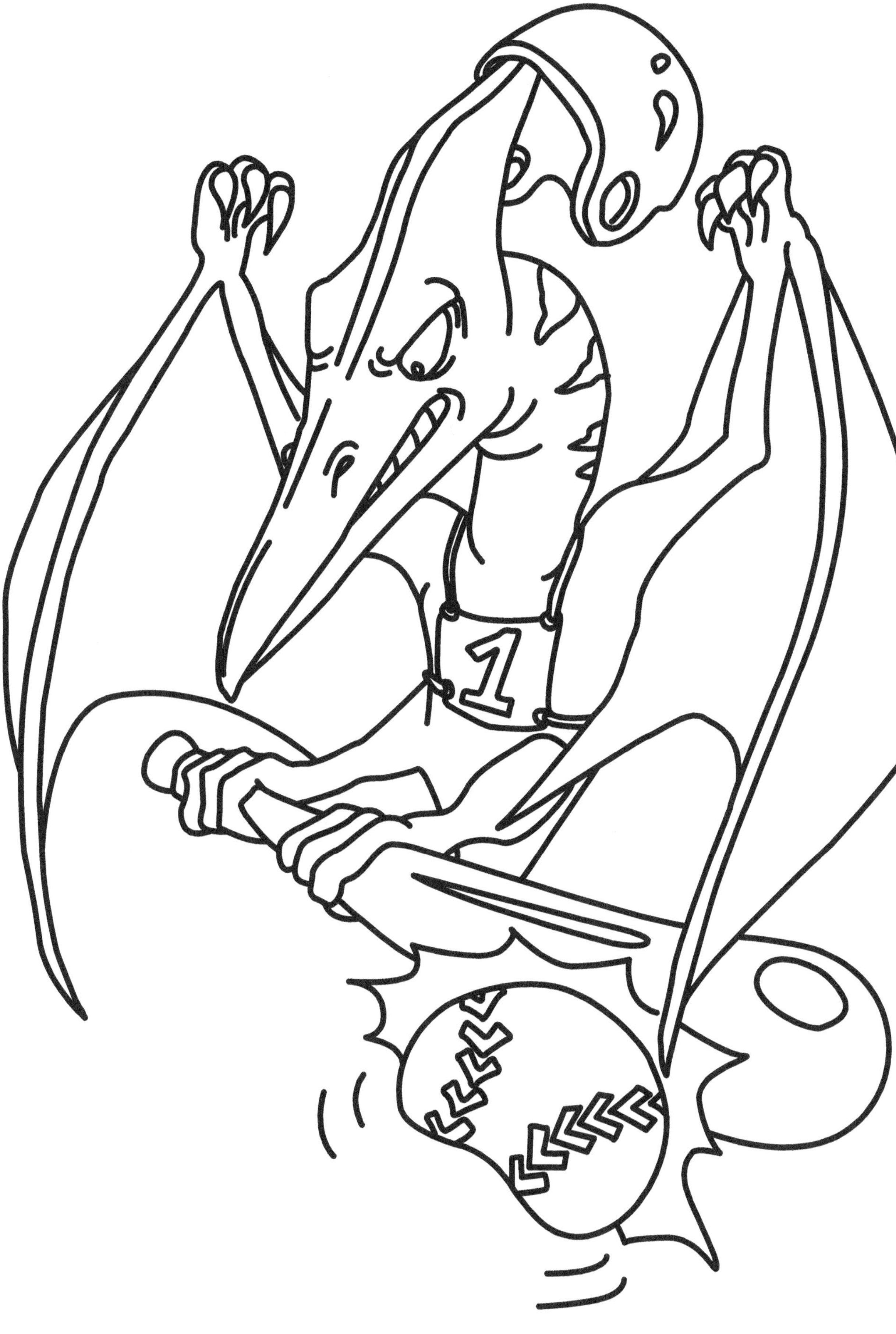
1

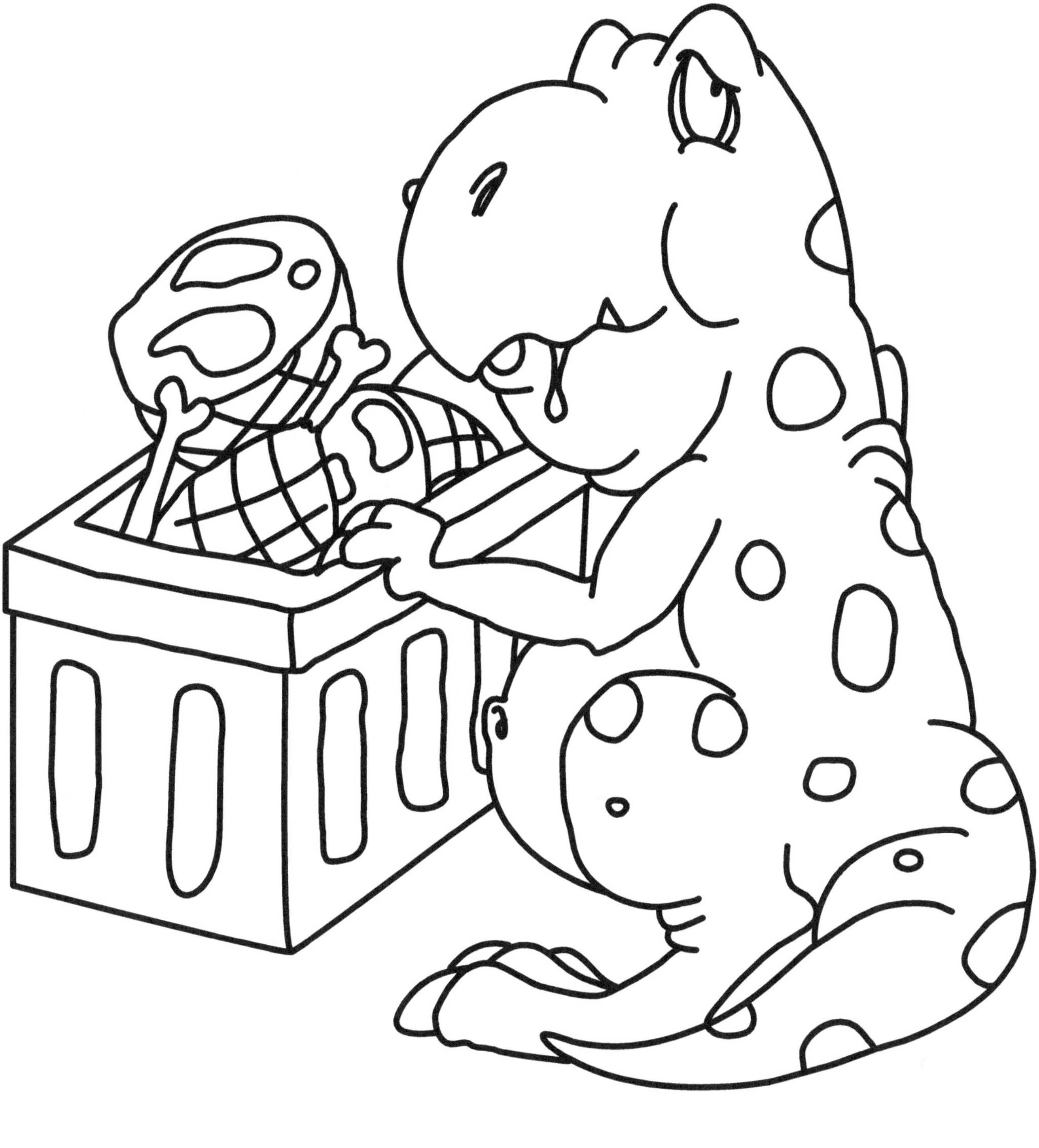

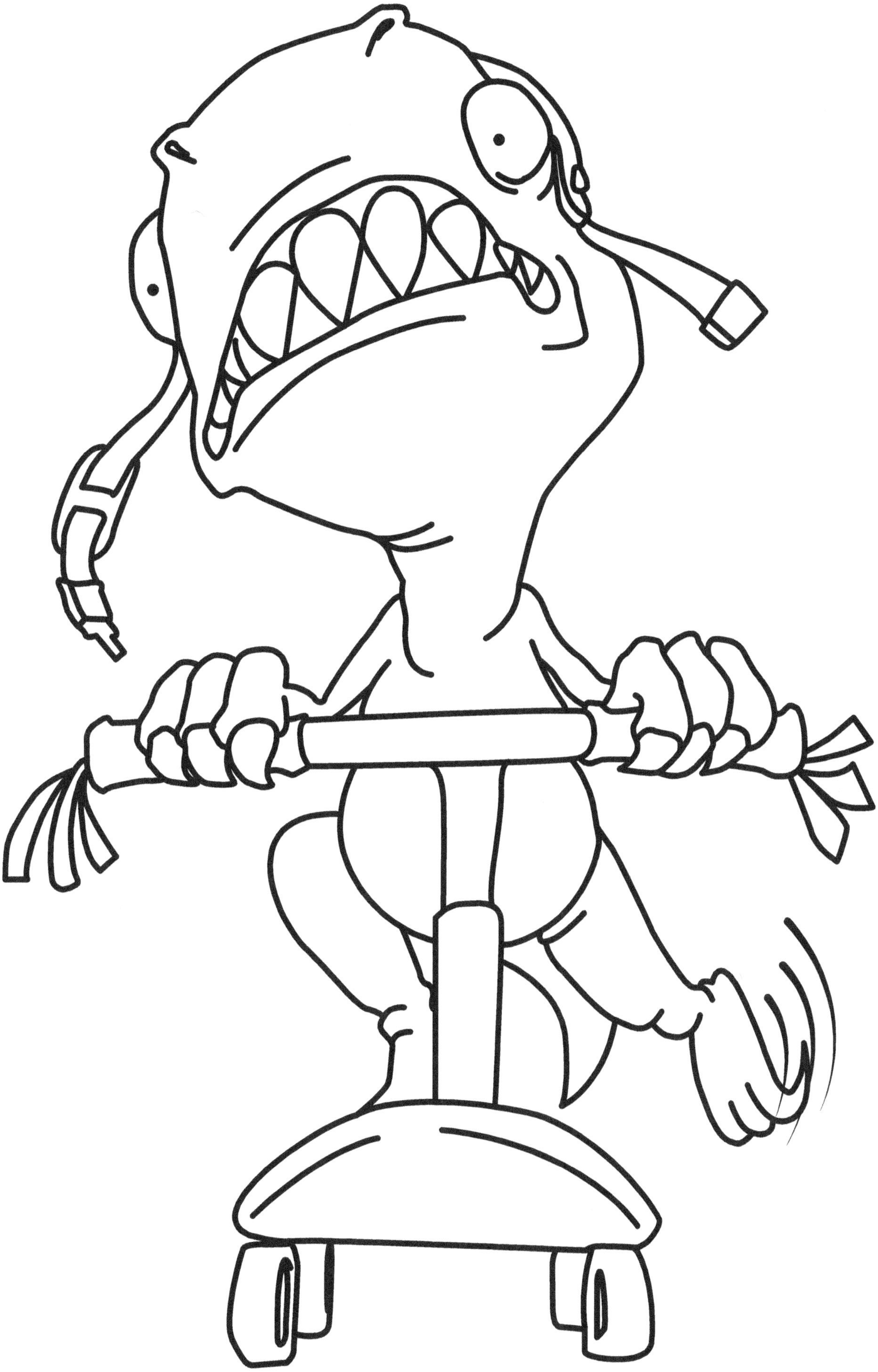

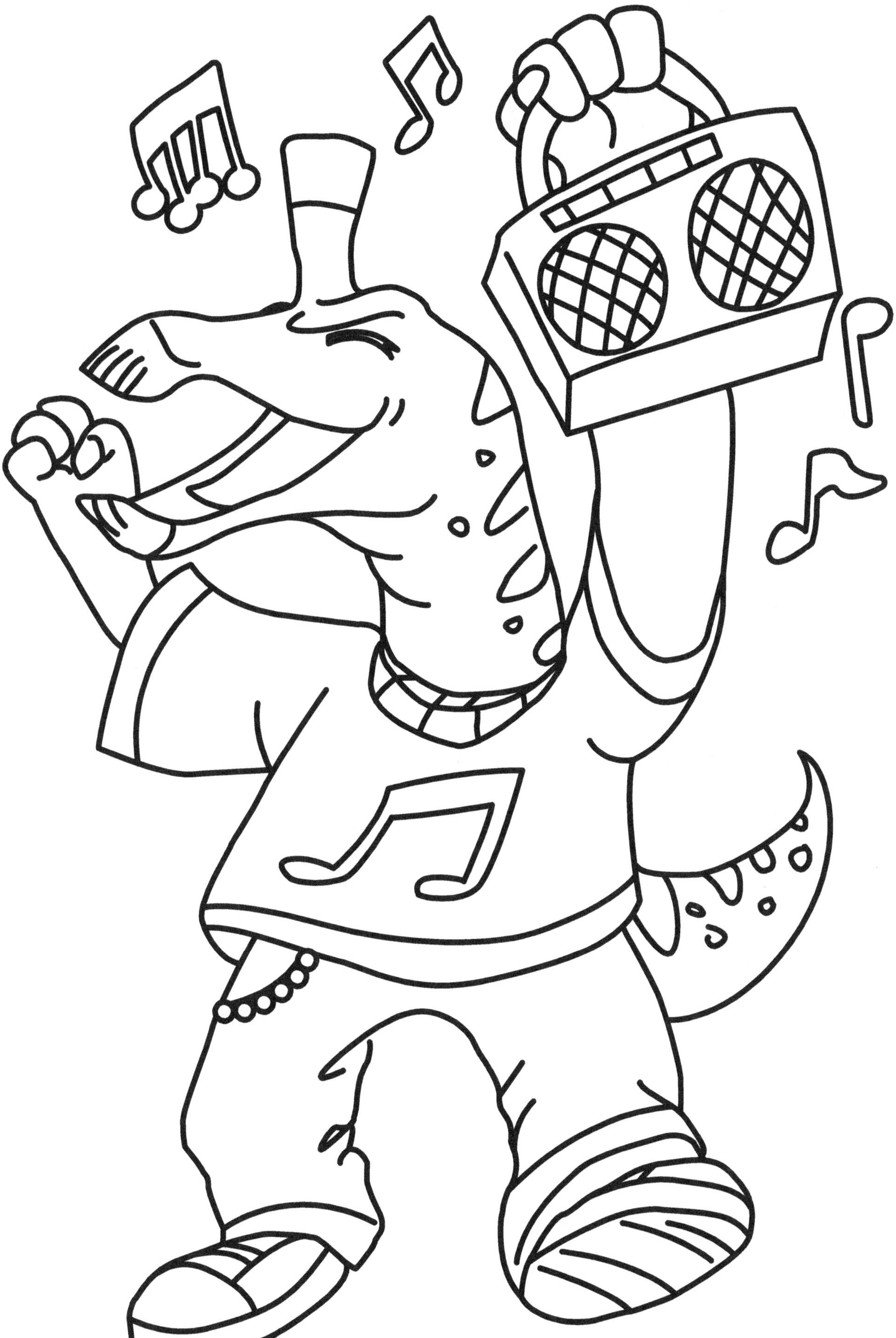

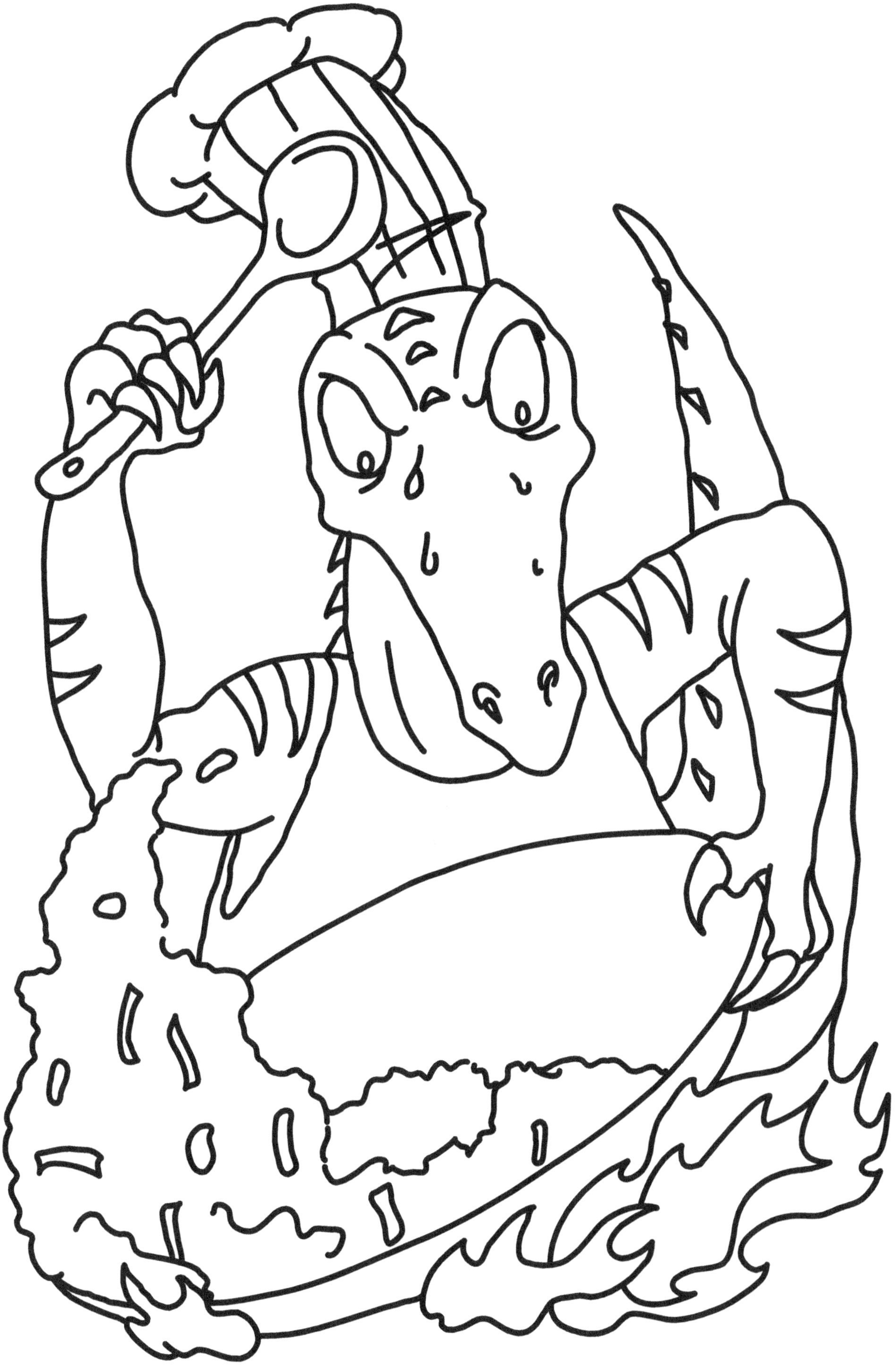

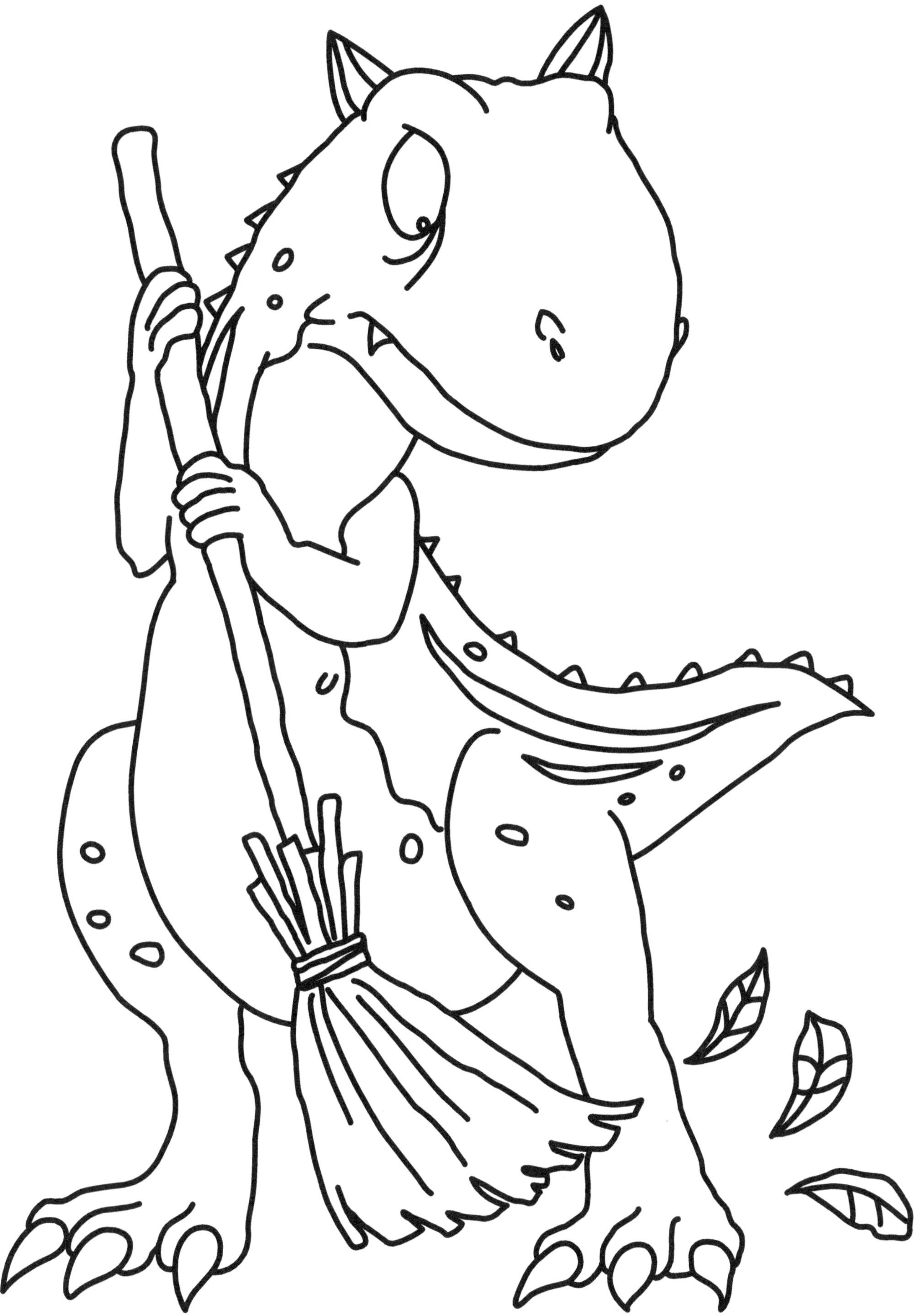

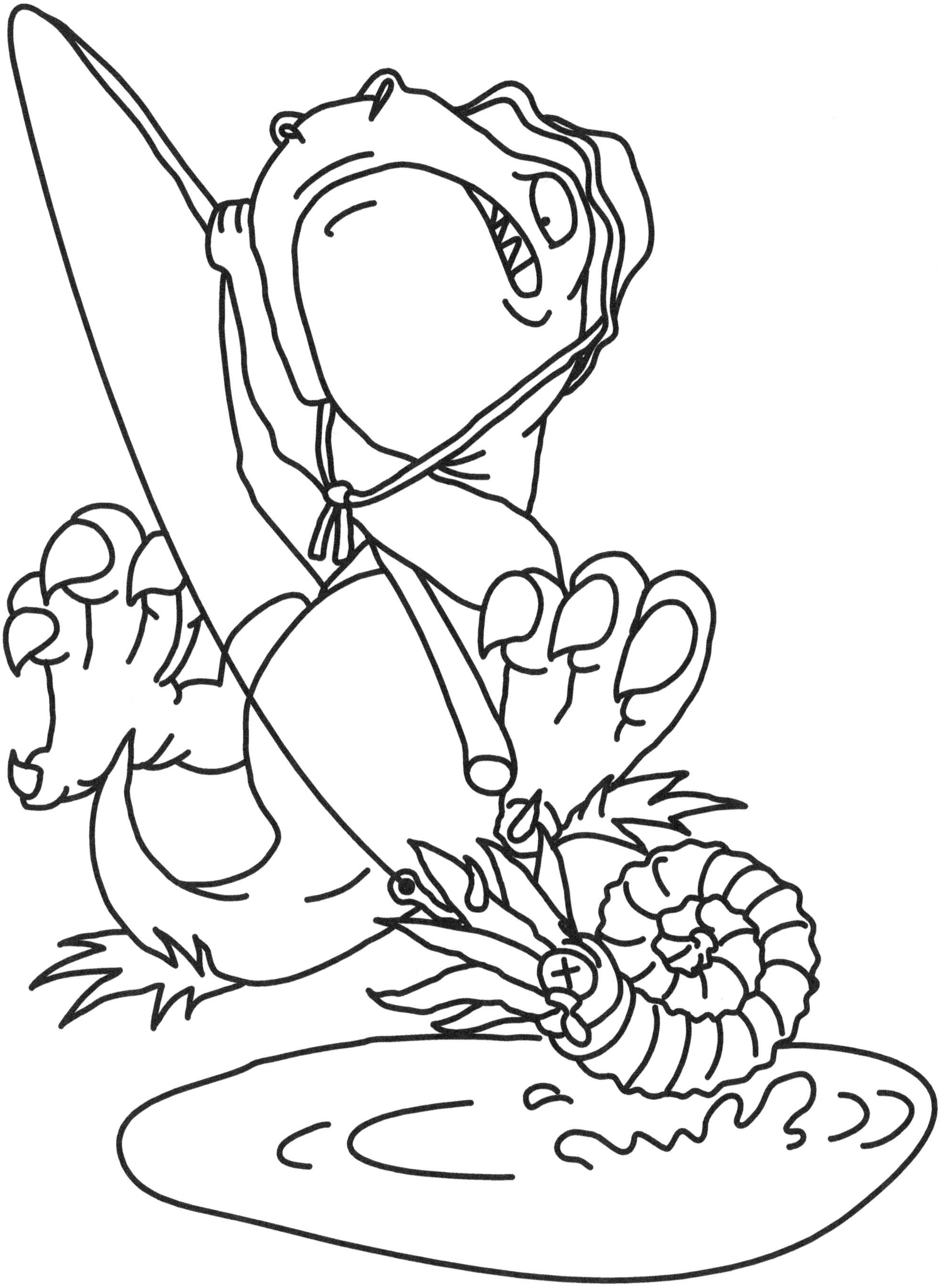

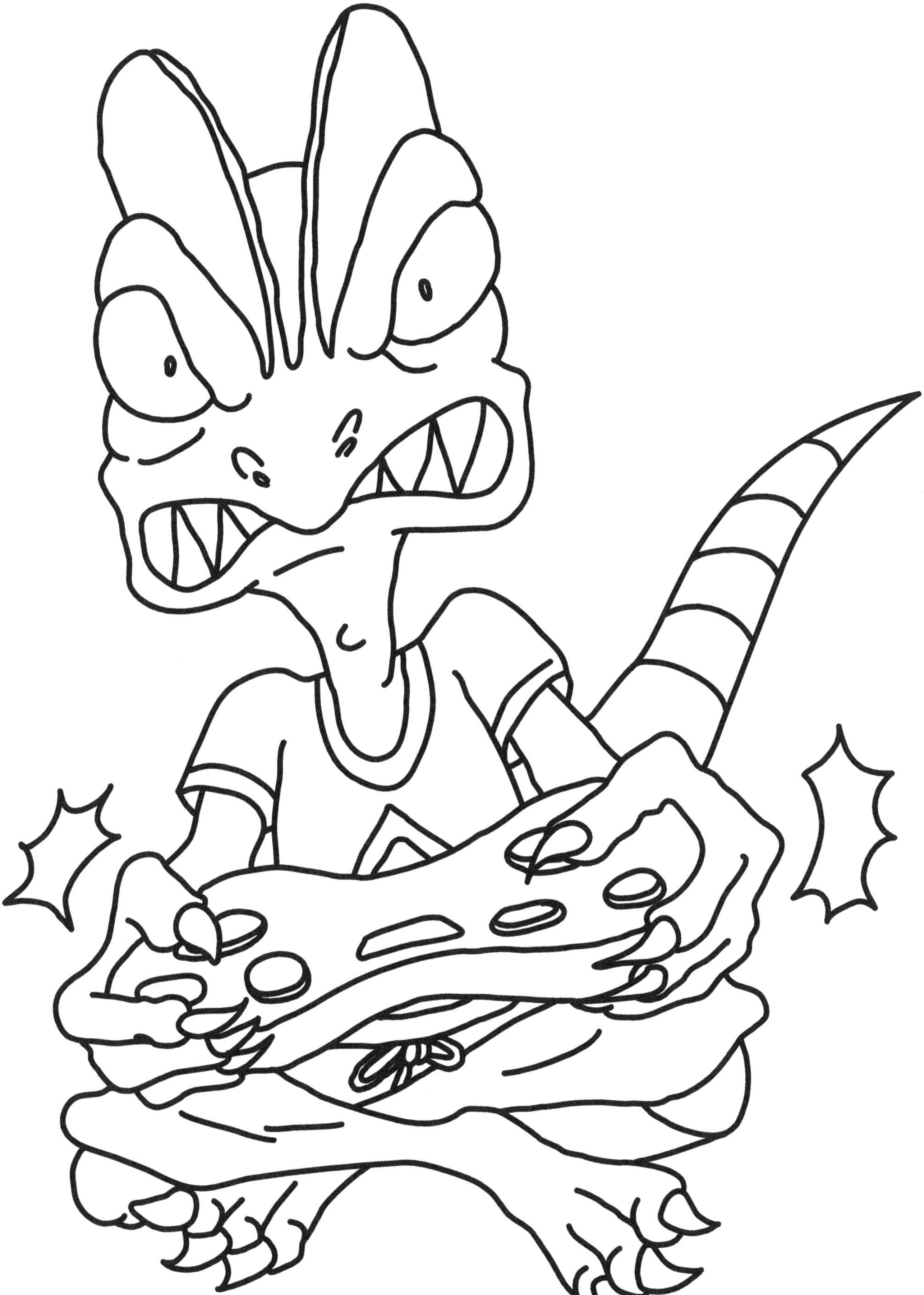

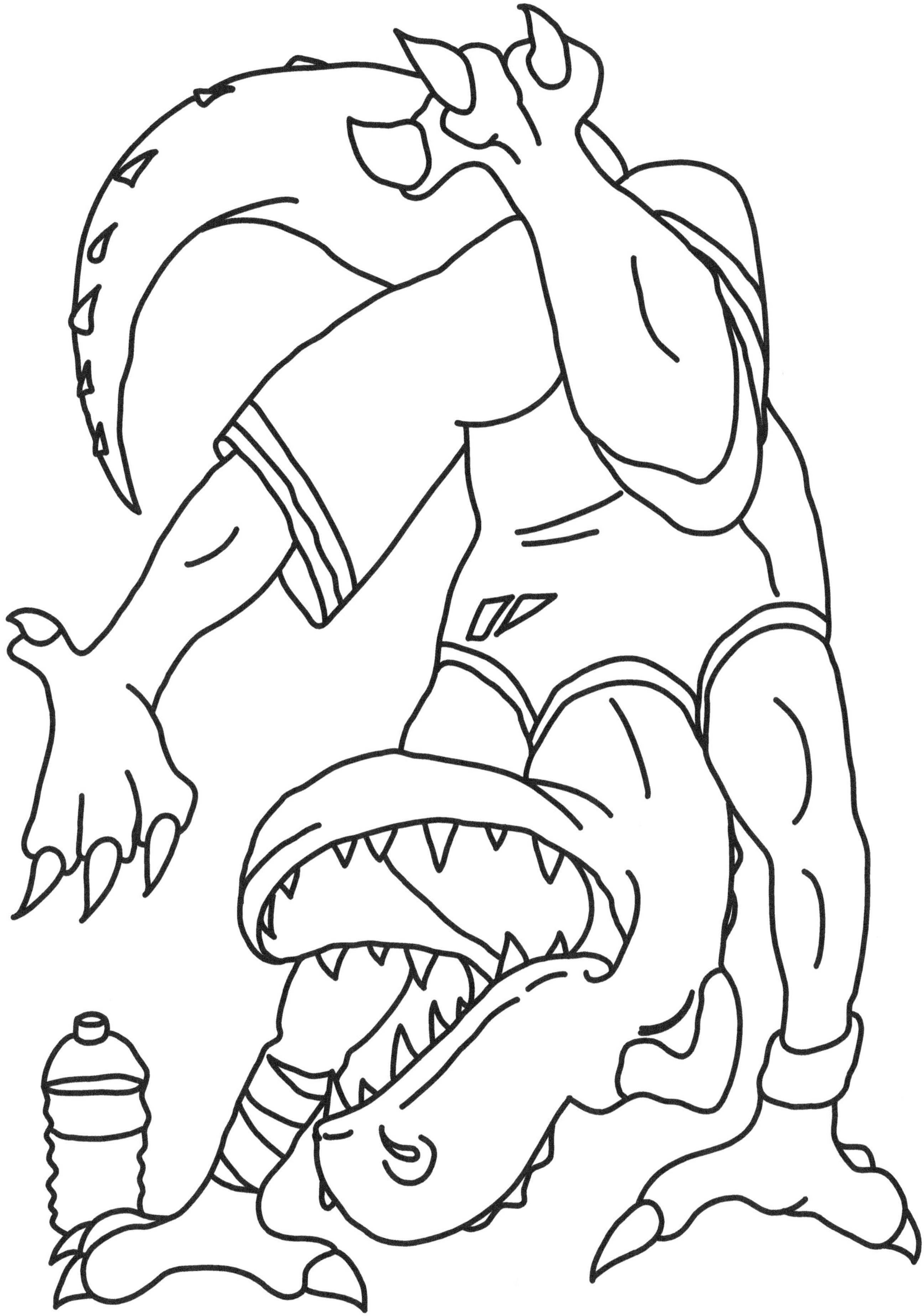

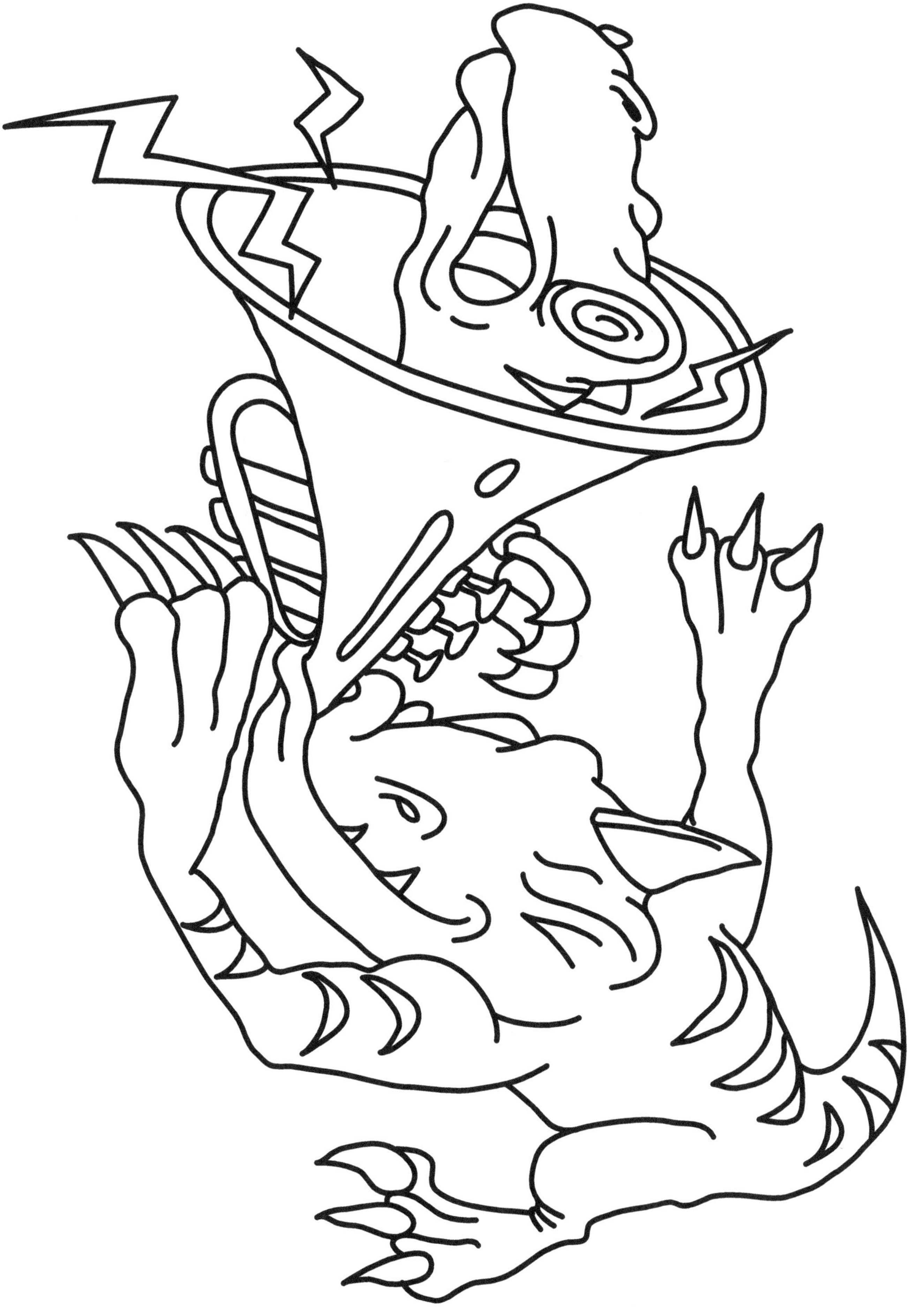

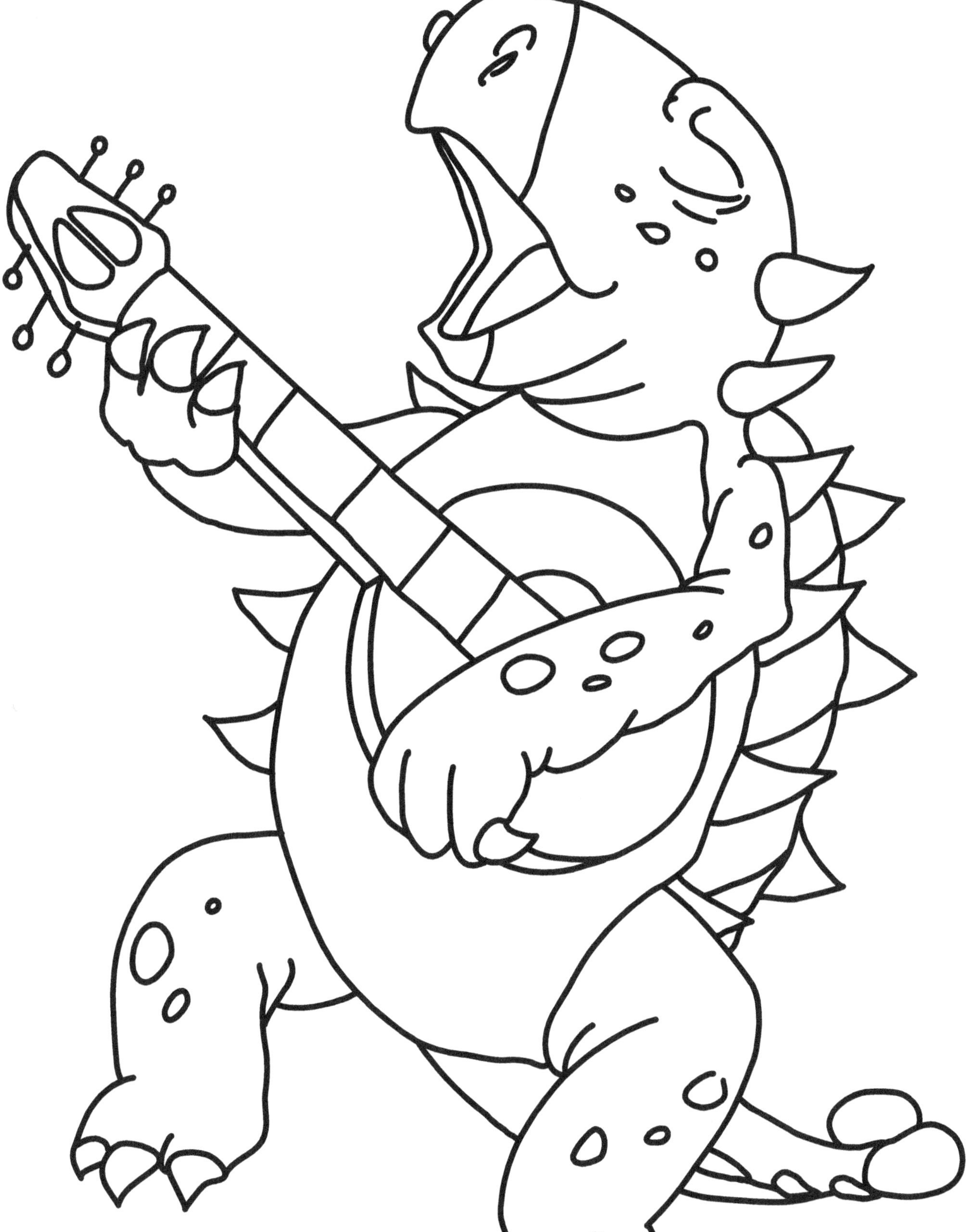

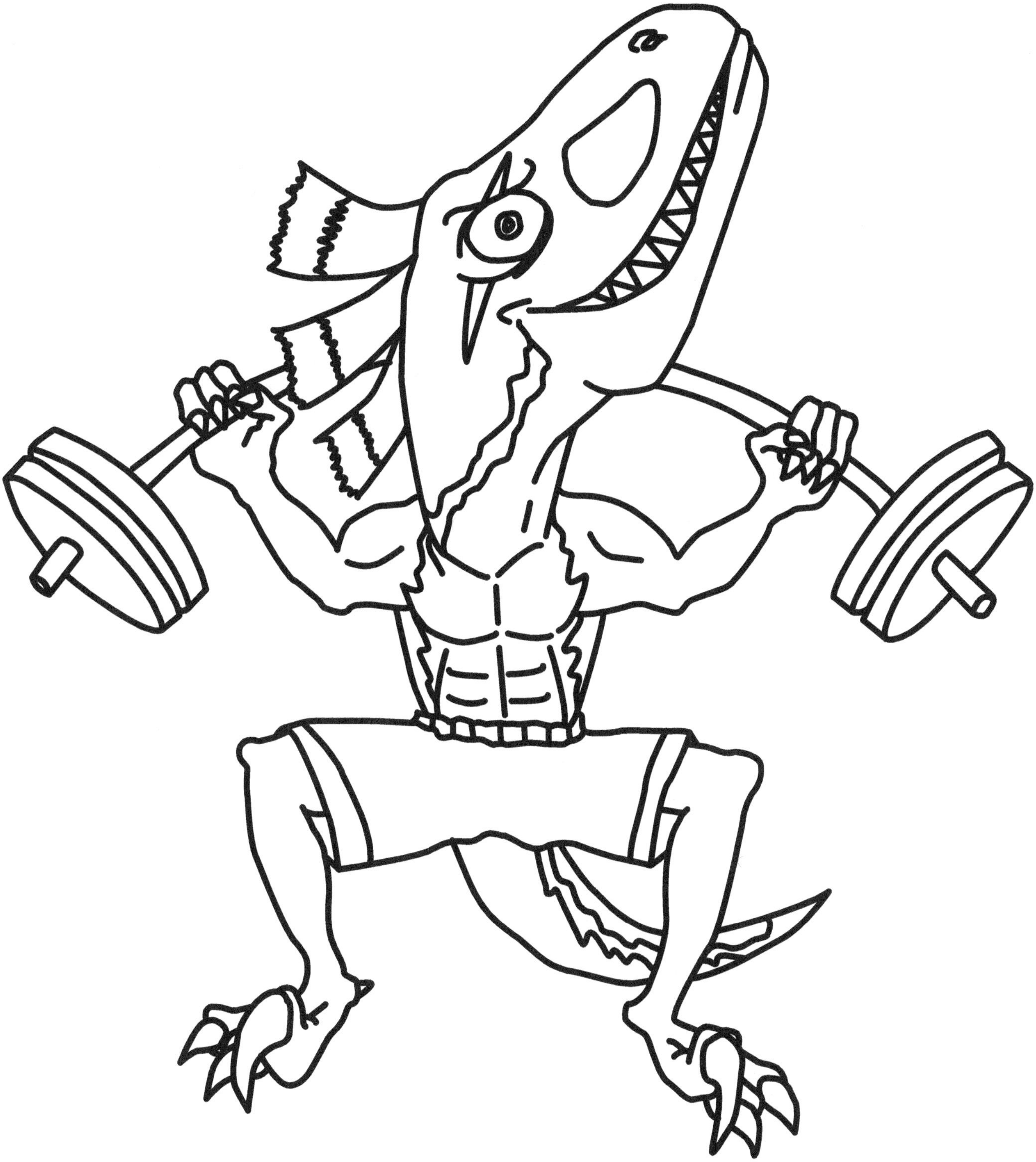

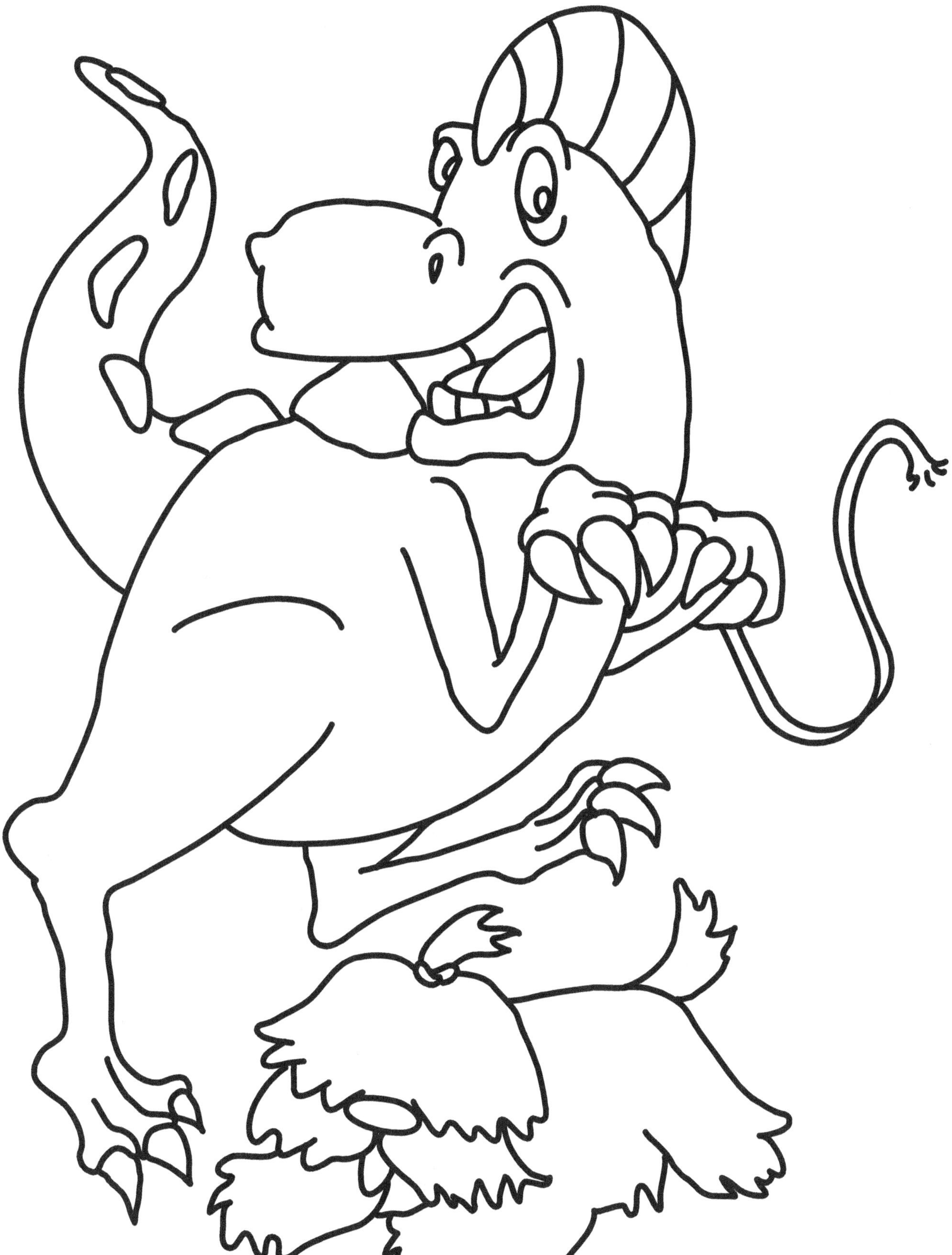

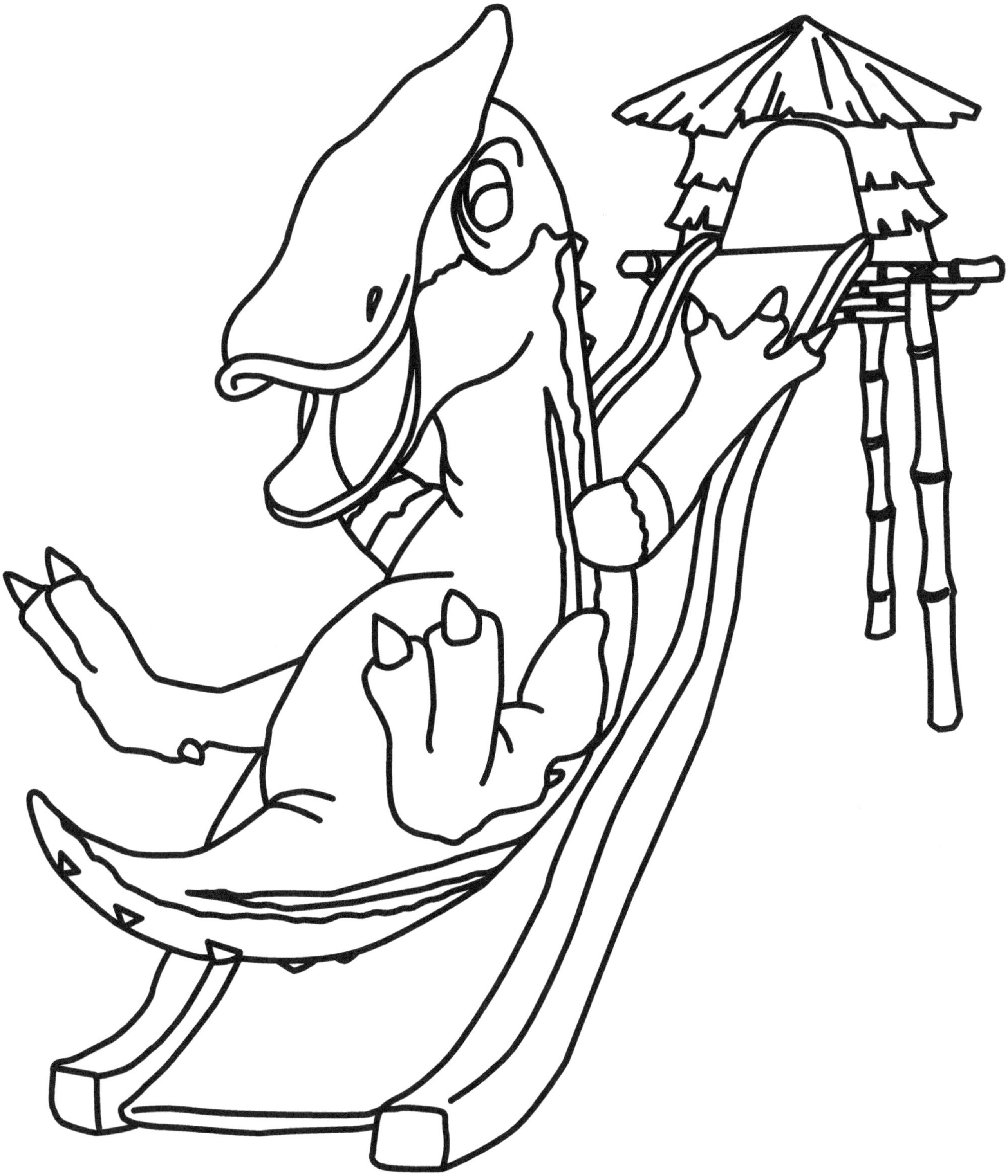

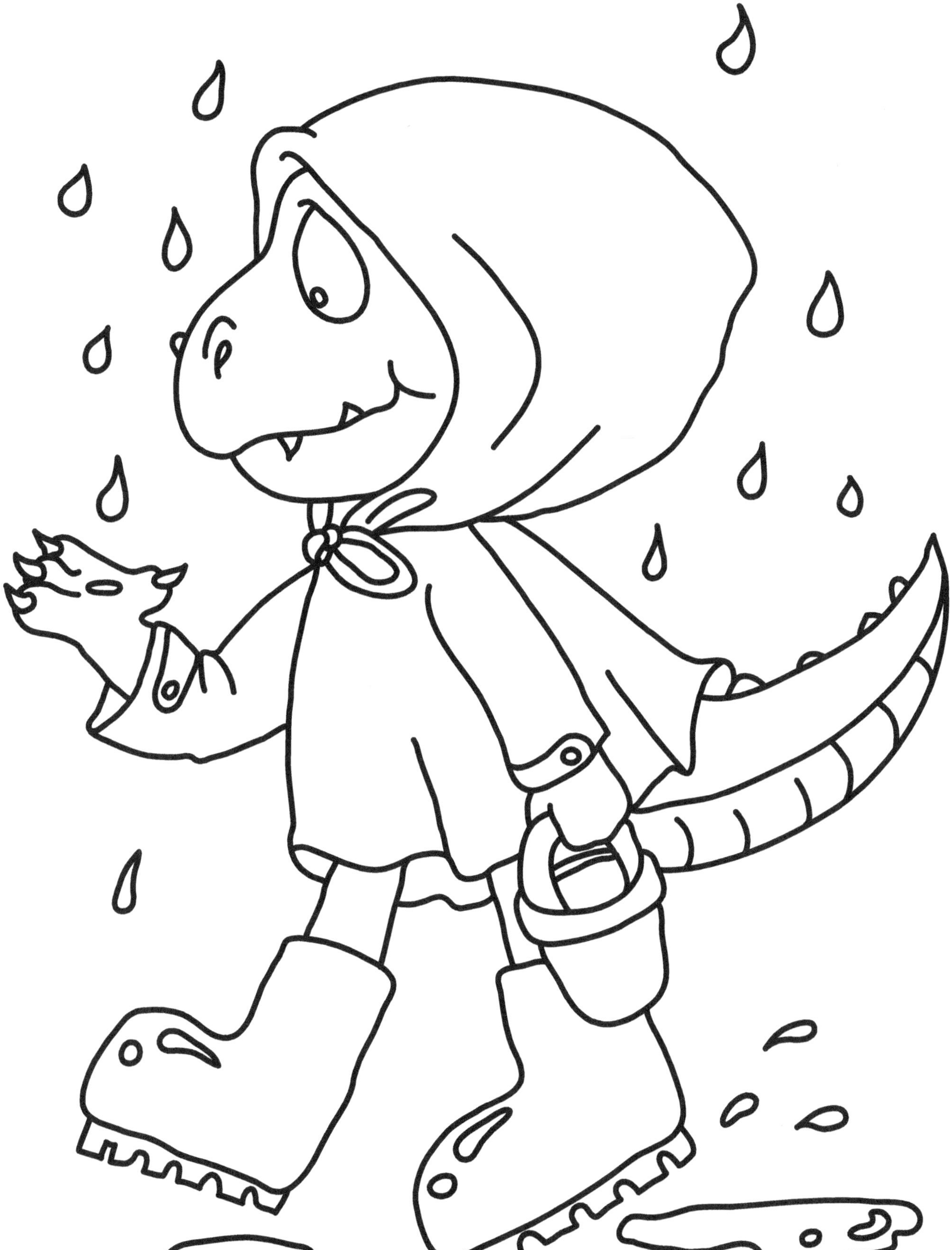

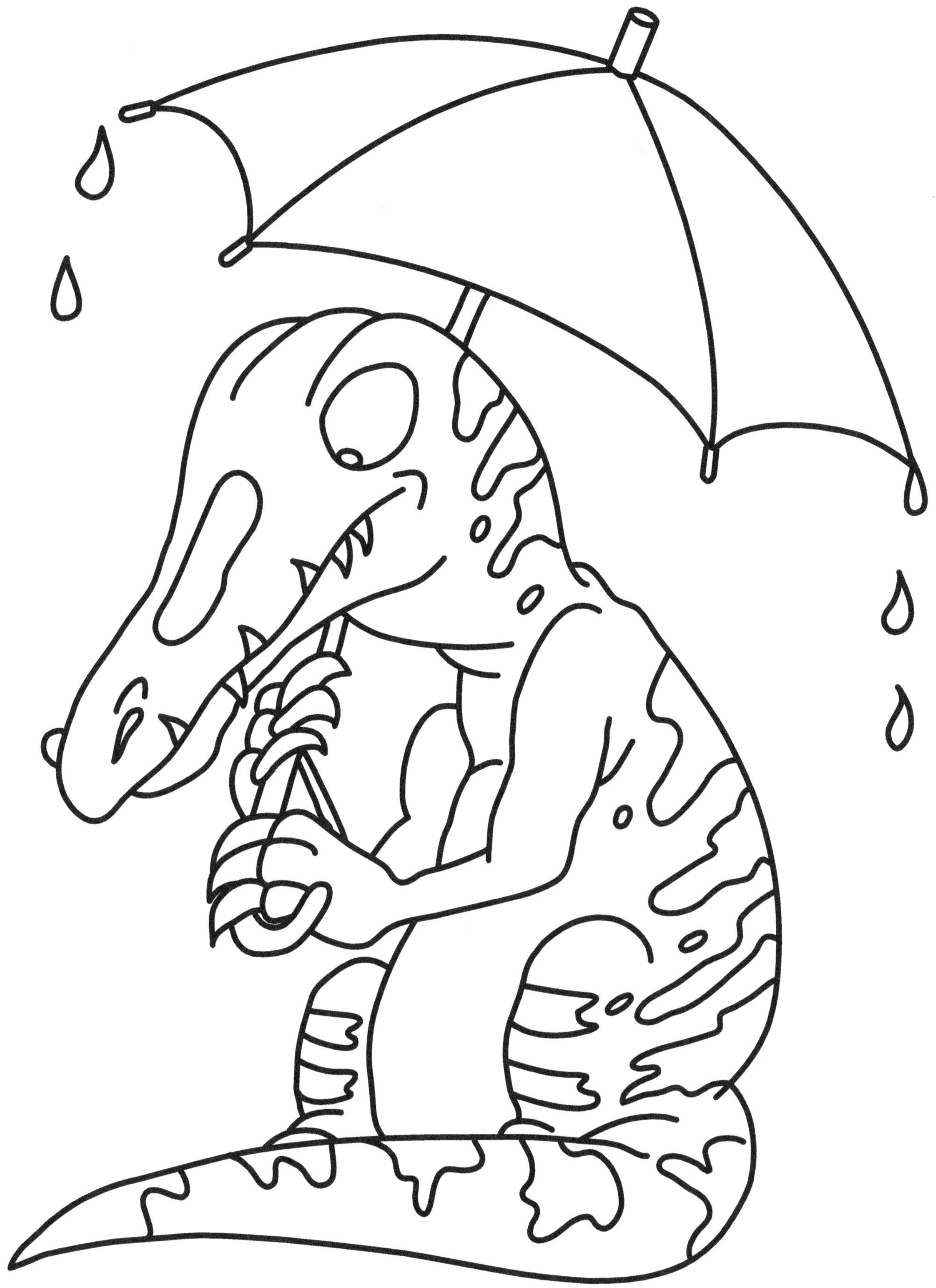

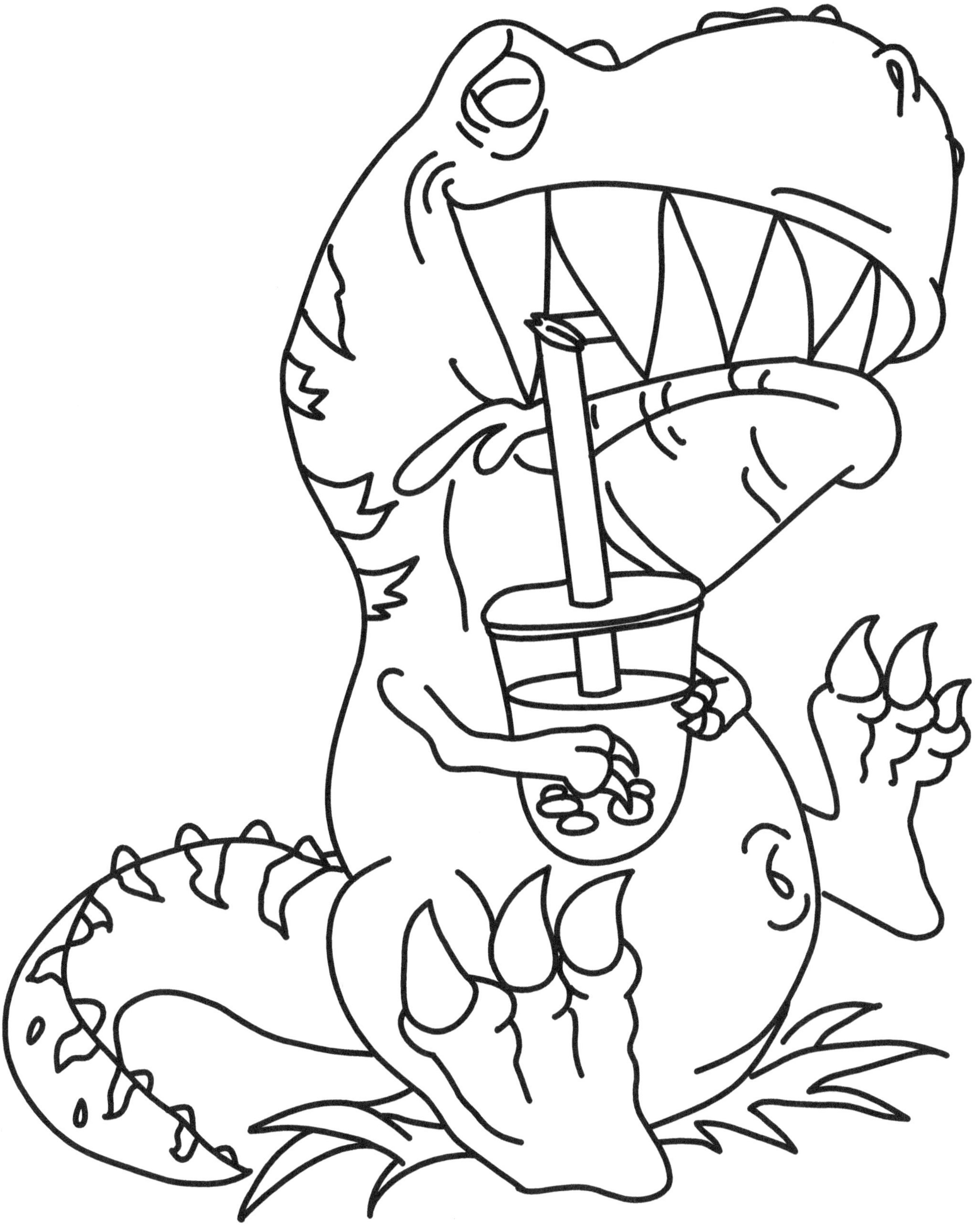

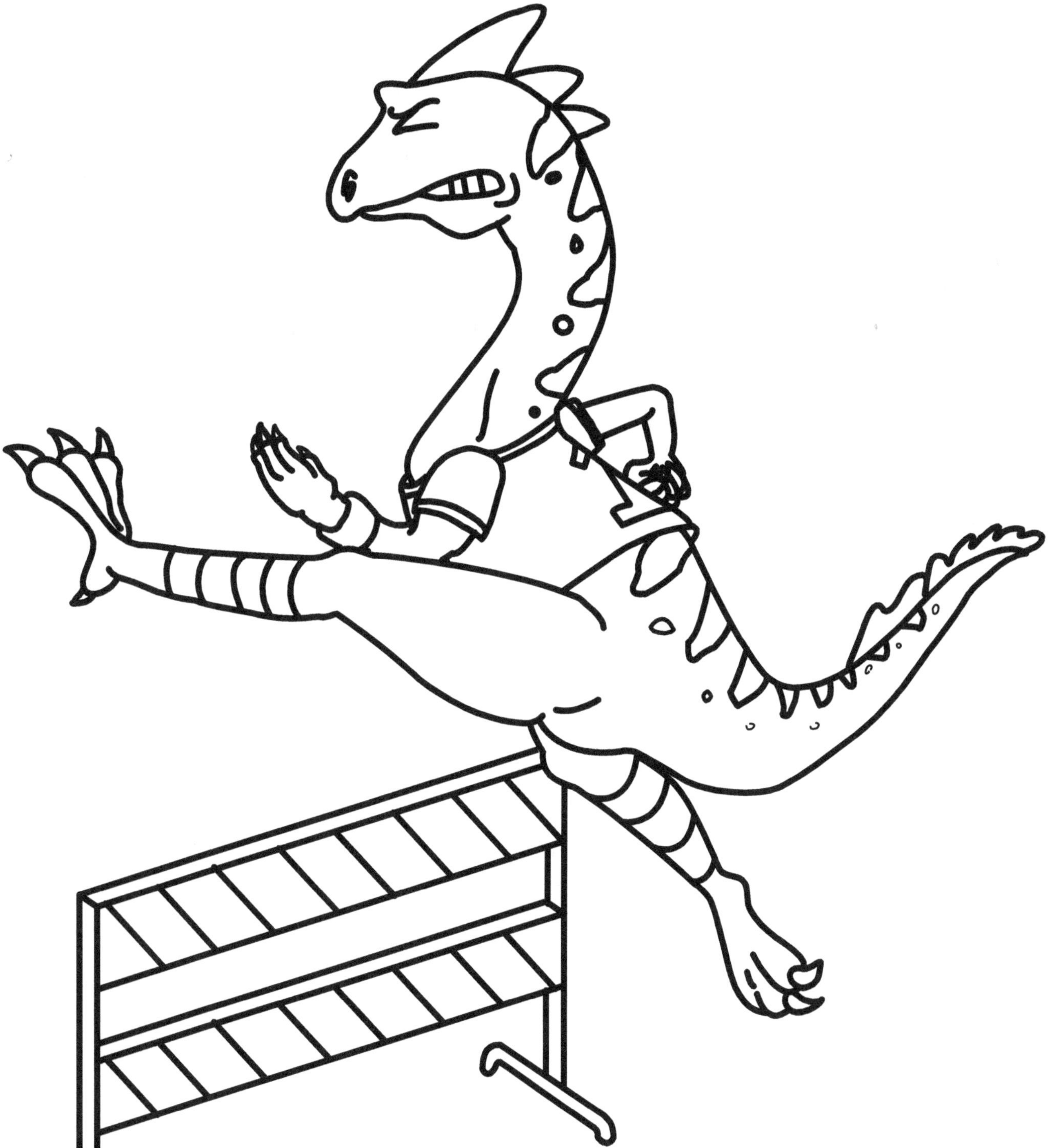

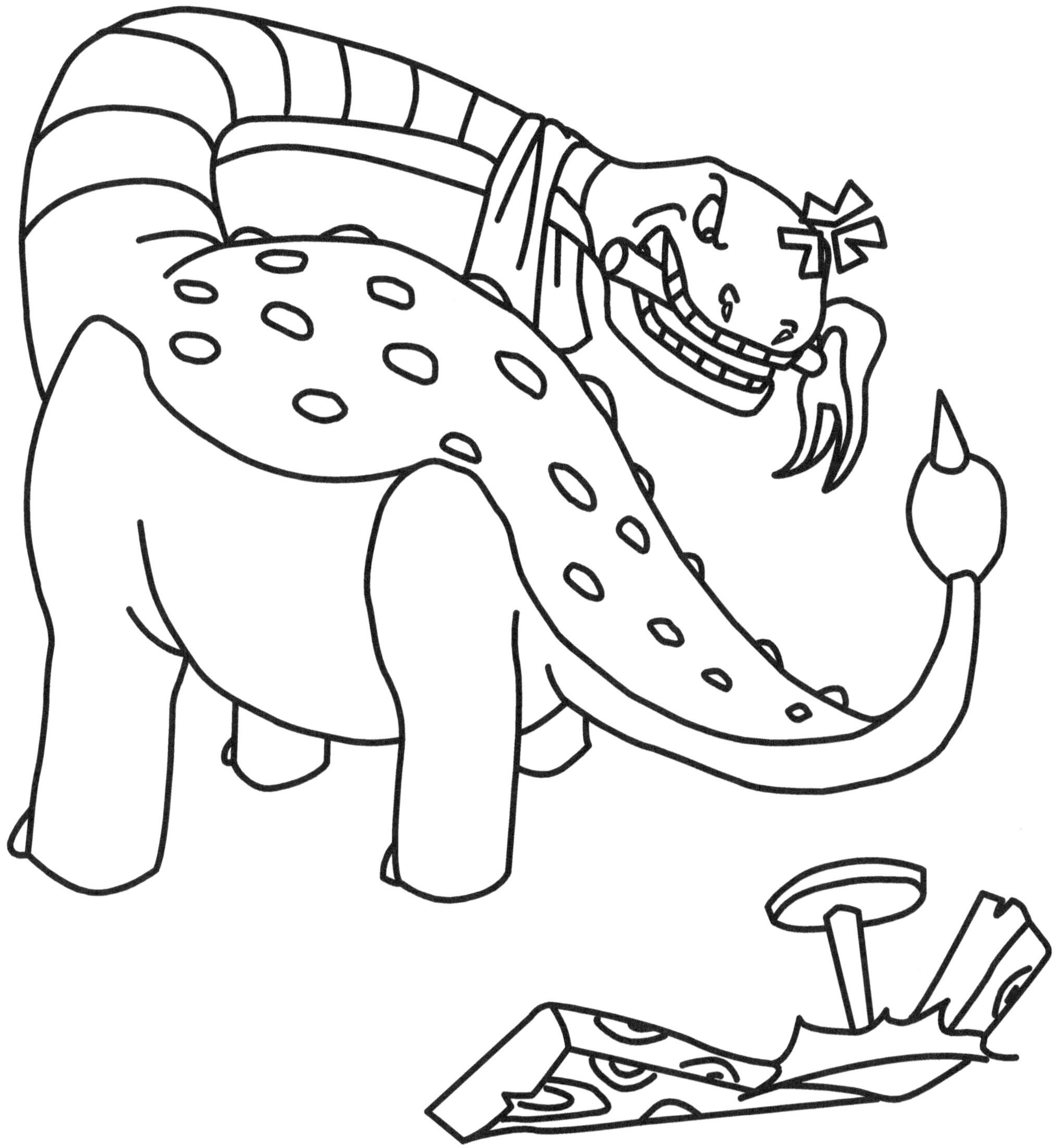

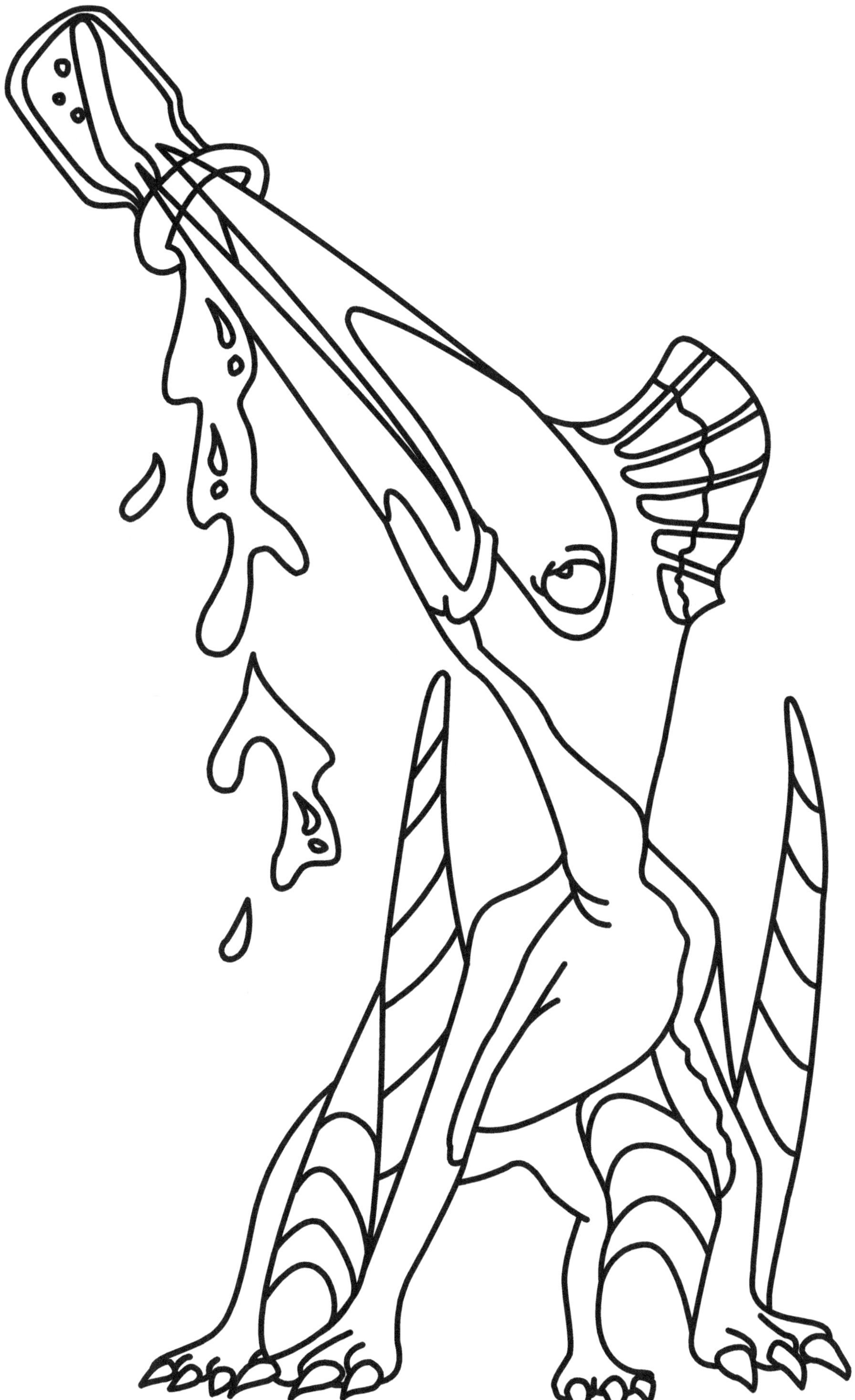

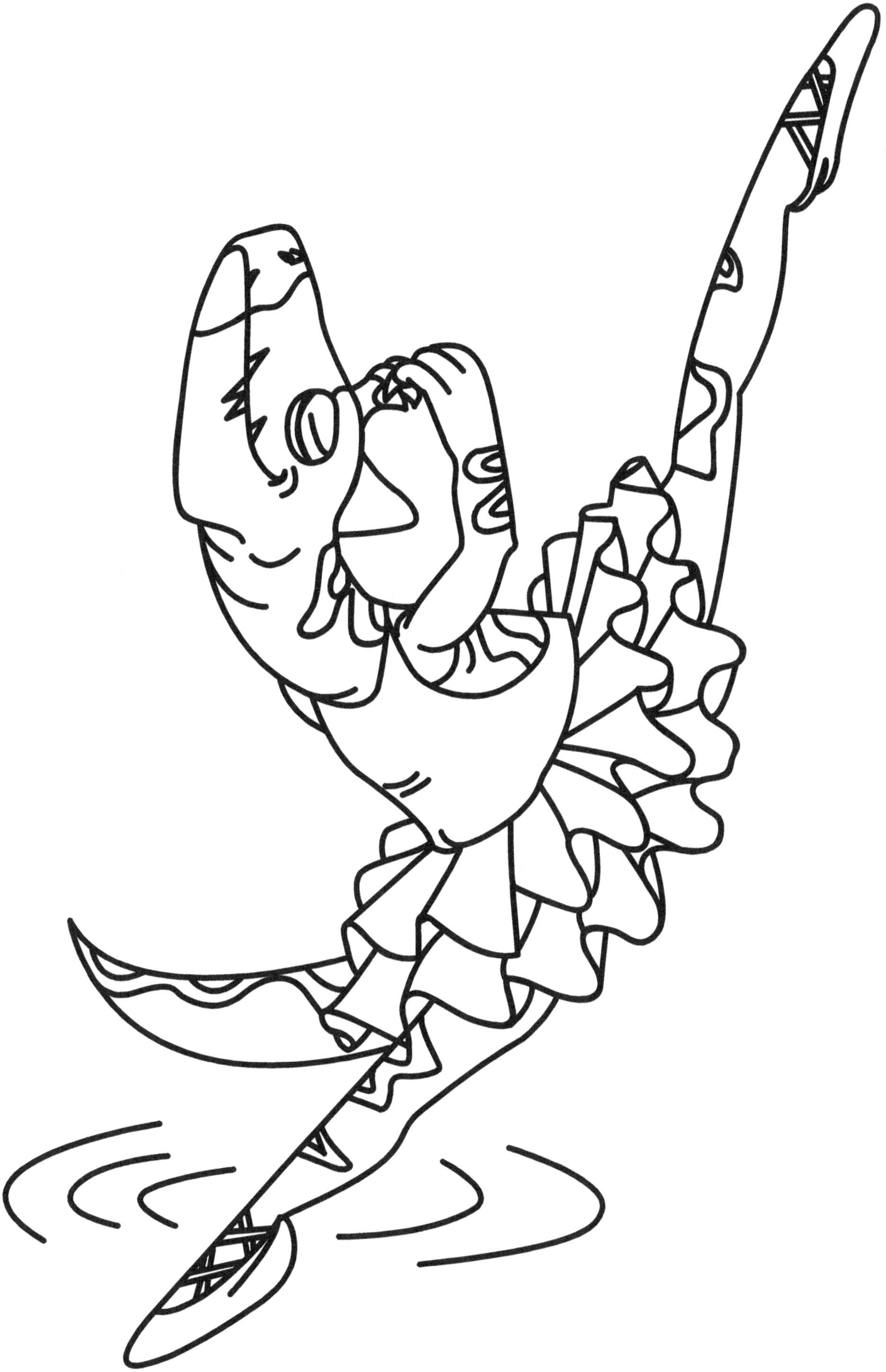

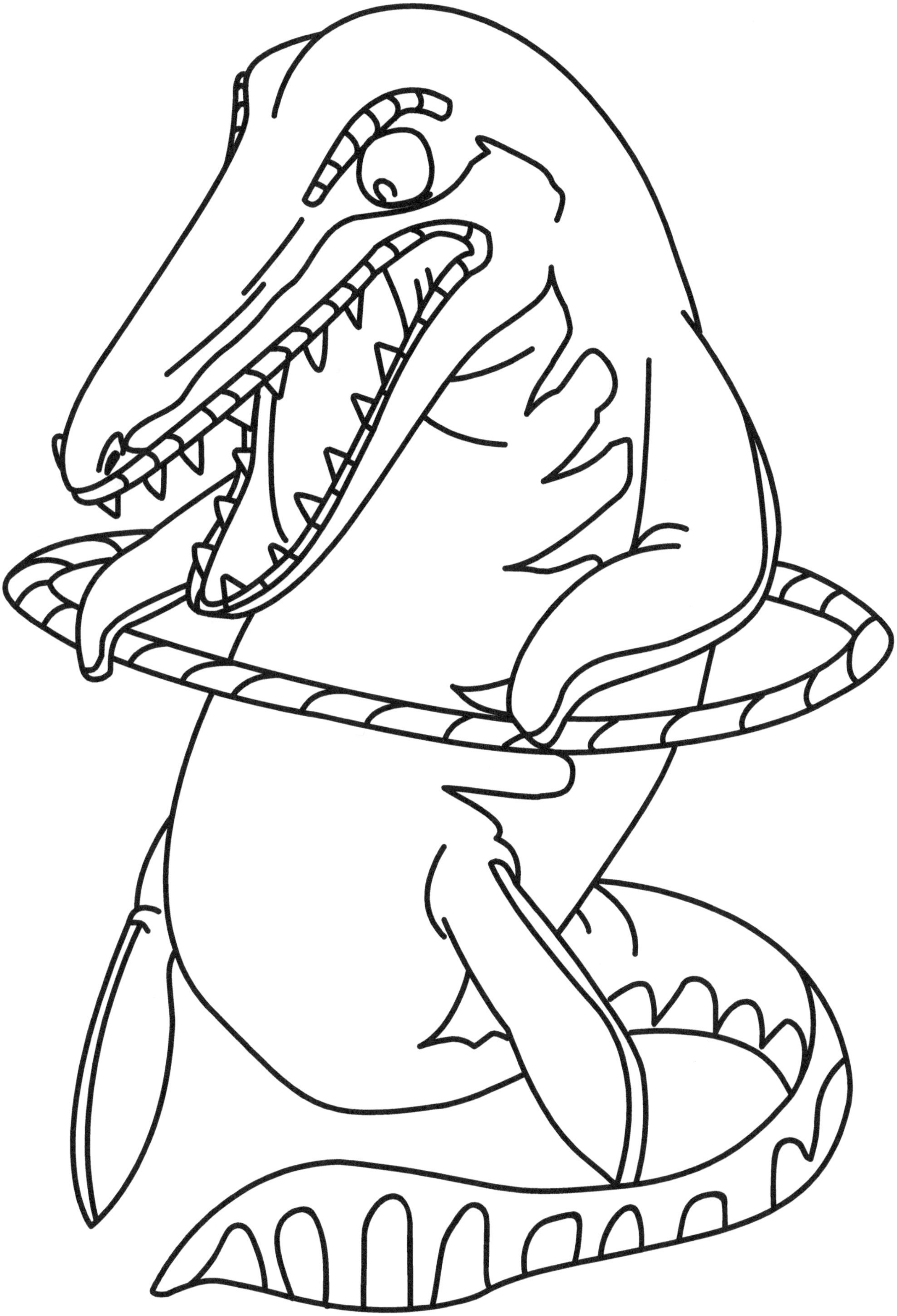

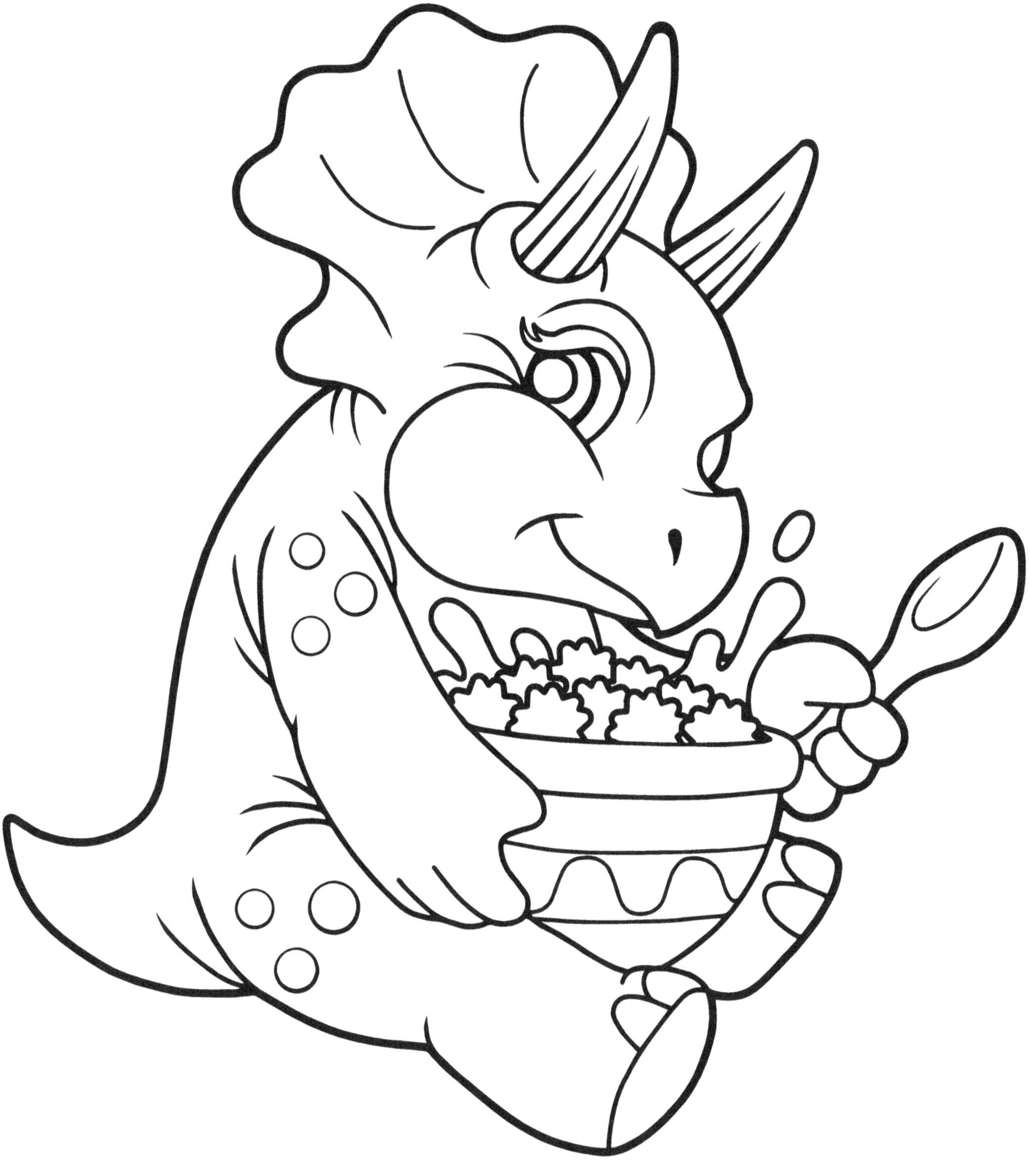

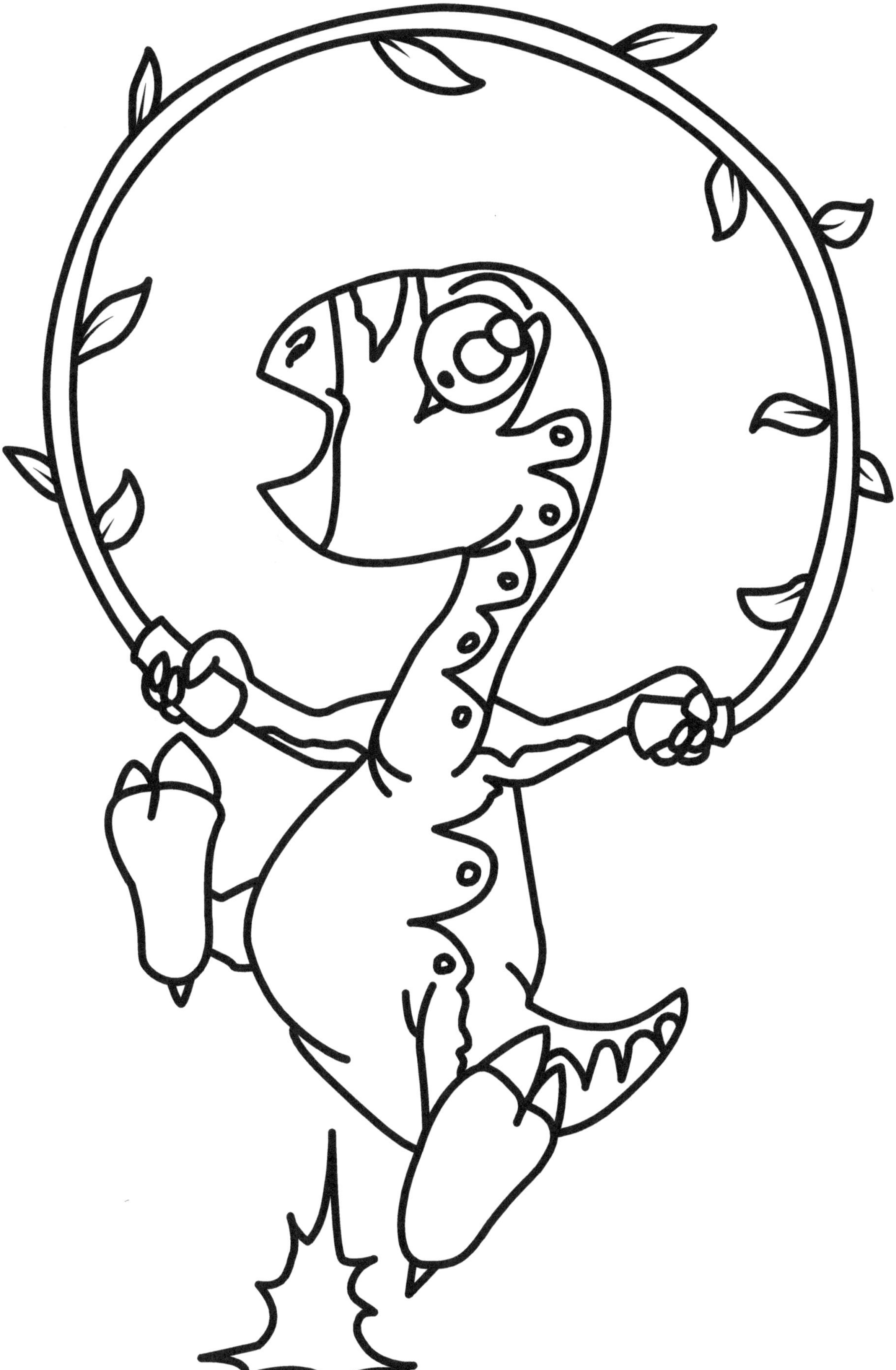

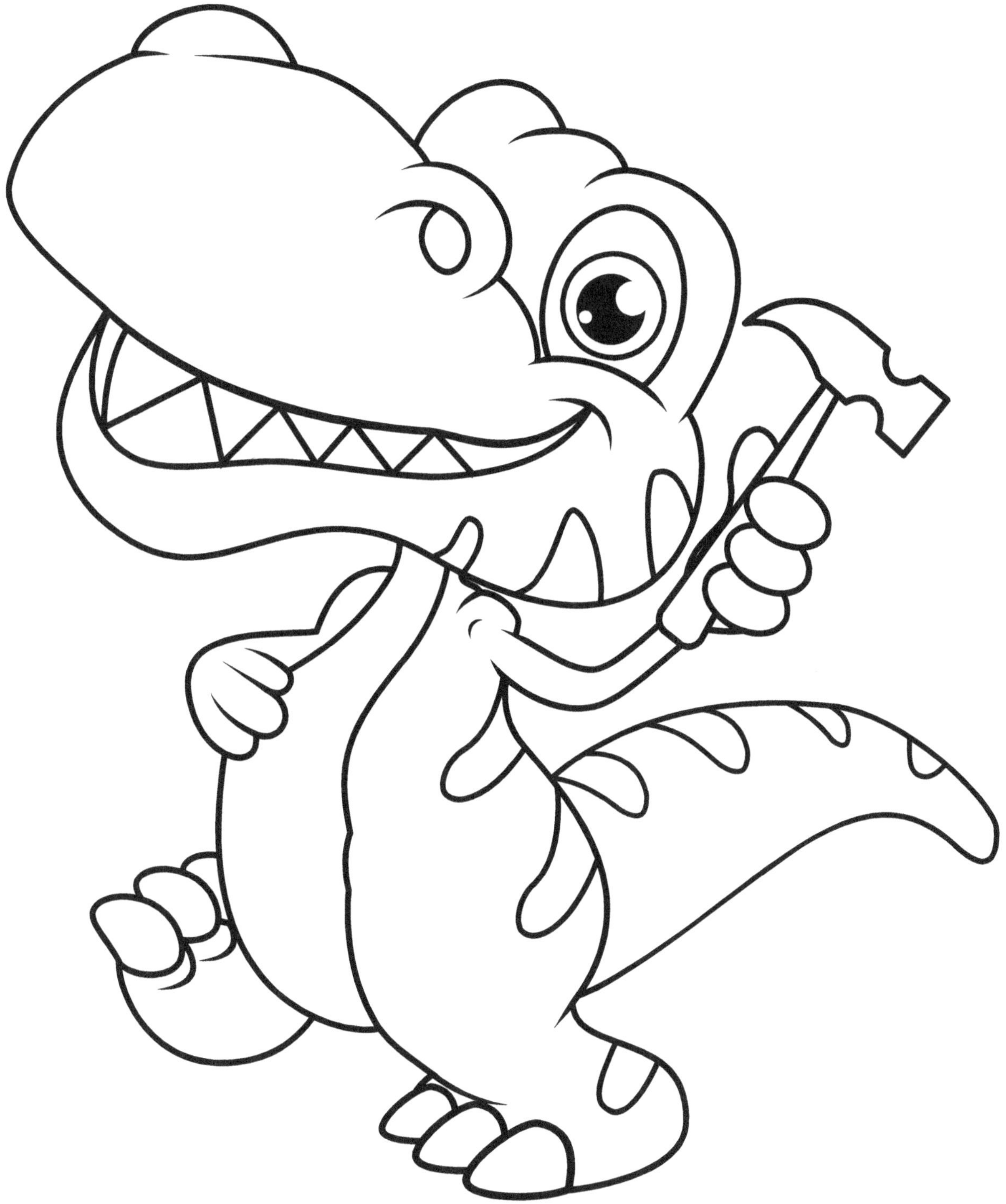

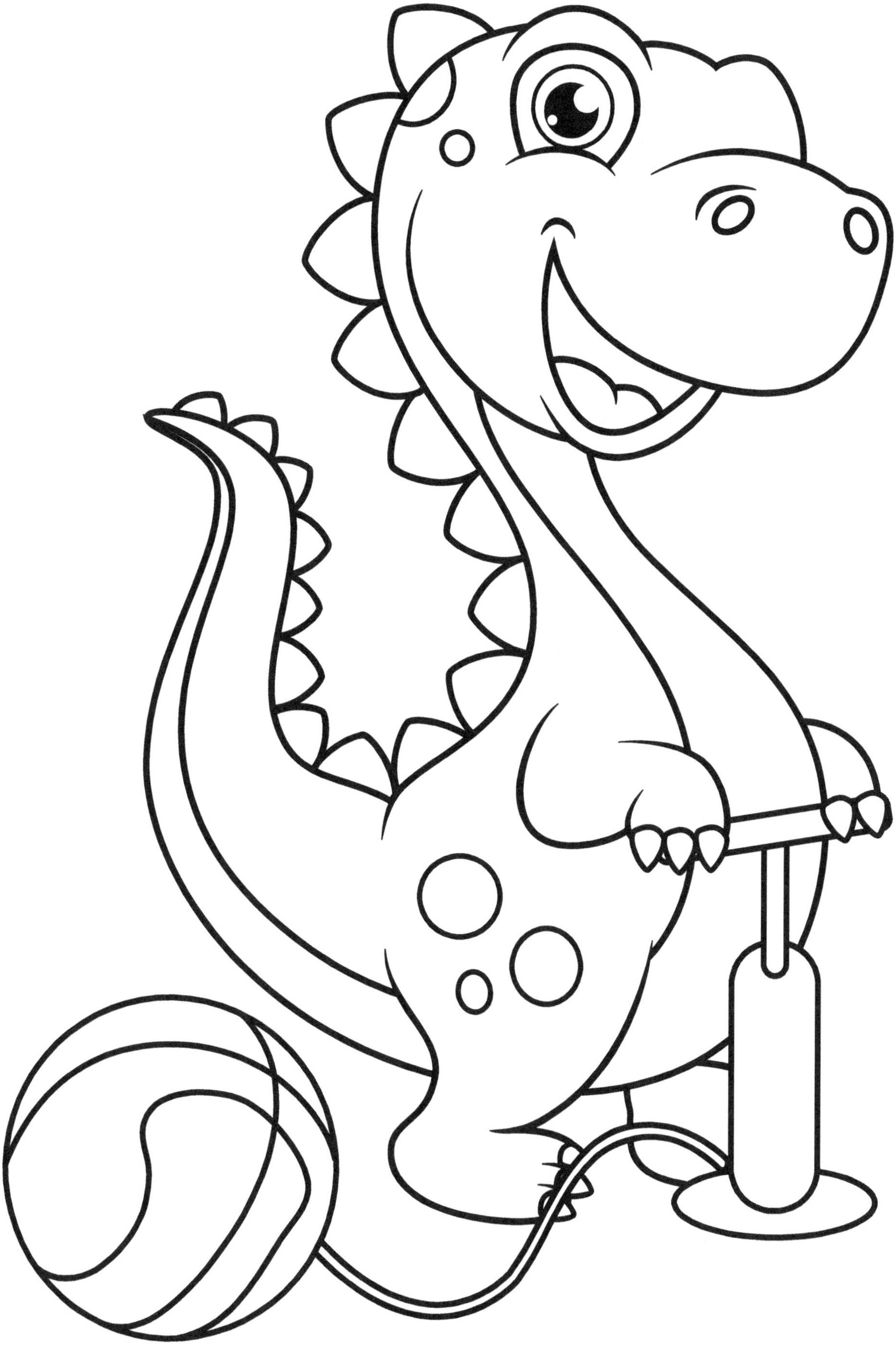

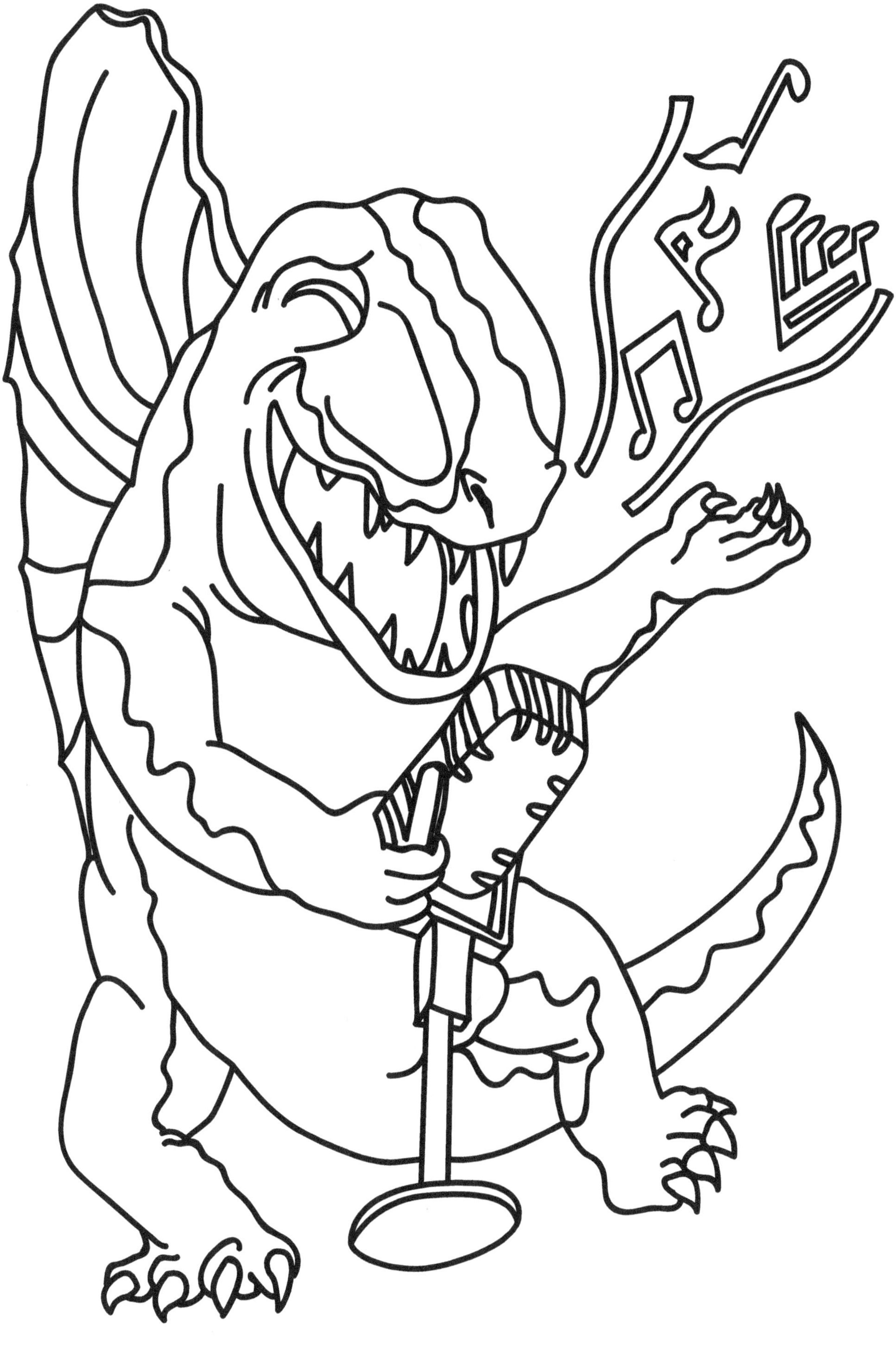

Author/ Lita Lovett Norrie

www.ingramcontent.com/pod-product-compliance
Lightning Source LLC
Chambersburg PA
CBHW081446220526
45466CB00008B/2521
9781672179904